Independent
Writing

I read and walked for miles at night along the beach, writing bad blank verse and searching endlessly for someone wonderful who would step out of the darkness and change my life. It never crossed my mind that that person could be me.

—Anna Quindlen

Independent Writing

One Teacher—Thirty-Two Needs, Topics, and Plans

M. Colleen Cruz

HEINEMANN
Portsmouth, NH

Heinemann
A division of Reed Elsevier Inc.
361 Hanover Street
Portsmouth, NH 03801–3912
www.heinemann.com

Offices and agents throughout the world

Library of Congress Cataloging-in-Publication Data
Cruz, Maria Colleen.
    Independent writing : one teacher—thirty-two needs, topics, and plans / M. Colleen Cruz.
      p. cm.
    Includes bibliographical references and index.
    ISBN 0-325-00540-0 (alk. paper)
    1. English language—Composition and exercises—Study and teaching (Elementary).
2. Creative writing (Elementary education).   3. Individualized instruction.   I. Title.

LB1576.C844 2004
372.62'3—dc22   2003020268

Editor: Kate Montgomery
Production coordinator: Elizabeth Valway
Production service: Denise Botelho
Cover photo: Angela Jimenez
Interior photos on pages ii, xx, 15, 31, 46, 61, 63, 72, 92, 99, 111, 122, 137, 139, 148 by Angela Jimenez.
Photos on pages 27, 55, 94, 127 by Colleen Cruz.
Cover design: Suzanne Heiser, Night & Day Design
Composition: Kim Arney Mulcahy
Manufacturing: Steve Bernier

Printed in the United States of America on acid-free paper
08 07 06 05 04 RRD 1 2 3 4 5

To all the P.S. 321 fourth graders I had the good fortune to teach and learn from.
You are the reason I wrote this book.

Contents

Foreword   ix

Acknowledgments   xi

Introduction   xv

1   Getting Started   1

2   Finding and Using Mentors in the Independent Workshop   47

3   When the Writer's Notebook Becomes the Writer's Notebook   73

4   The Writing Colony: Building Community for Independent Writers   93

5   Trouble!   123

6   Taking Stock and Moving Forward: Assessment and Planning
    Writing Lives   149

Afterword   175

Bibliography   177

Index   179

Foreword

When I began writing as my full-time job several months ago, my husband would come home from his work each day and ask me, somewhat jokingly, "So, how many pages did you write today?" At first, I enjoyed the question and found myself waiting anxiously for him to ask so I could say "seventeen" or "twenty-two" or "twelve." It was our little end-of-the-work-day ritual.

And then I had a really bad writing day.

"Why do you always ask me that question?" I cried in distress. "Don't you understand I can't just crank out pages everyday? I'm not a machine! Don't you understand I have to *revise* sometimes?" But I hadn't been revising that day, actually. I just couldn't get things to work out right. I had stayed at my desk all day and had gotten nowhere. I felt defeated, and the defeat was all mine to own.

At its very core, writing is a supreme act of independence. The writer faces the blank page alone. She may bring with her the sound advice of an editor, the luxury of time, the passion of an idea, the encouragement of a strong writing community. But in the end, she alone must find the words she needs, get them down, and make them work together. If the writing goes well or badly or doesn't happen at all, she alone is responsible. There is no one else to credit; there is no one else to blame. The words belong to the writer who puts them down on that blank page.

Colleen Cruz knows this about writing. She has experienced it first hand as a writer of short stories and novels, as a member of writing groups, and as someone simply "in love with the act of writing." She came to know about independence first as a writer, but now she knows about it as a *teacher* of writing as well, and we will all benefit from what she knows and shares in this wonderful book, *Independent Writing*.

Working from the essential premise that students need "to learn to become independent as much as they need to learn the fundamentals of writing," Colleen invites us to spend a year in her fourth-grade classroom and watch, listen, and learn as she teaches her young students about independence by requiring them *to be* independent during their daily writing workshop. We see Colleen's students choose their own topics and genres, and then in project proposals decide when, where, and how they will publish the writing projects they will pursue. We watch as they find their own writing mentors, decide whether or not to join writing groups, and figure out on their own how they'll use their writers' notebooks to support their writing. We listen in as they respond to Colleen's teaching and to the writing of their classmates. We celebrate with them at year's end as they leave fourth grade—their cookbooks and novels and plays in tow—really understanding what it means to carry on with an independent writing life.

And through it all, we are privileged to "crawl inside" their teacher's head and know what she is thinking and *re*thinking as she figures out what she needs to do to support a room full of independent ten-year-old writers. Perhaps the greatest strength of *Independent Writing*, is that Colleen shares with such honesty what it's like to take a risk and teach on the very edge of her best understandings. In a world of quick fixes and easy answers, I am moved again and again by the integrity of her teaching.

When I first saw Colleen after reading the manuscript for *Independent Writing*, I told her that the book had the potential to change significantly the professional conversation about the teaching of writing. And I really believe this is true. When there is so much pressure to teach writing from programs that foster inherently dependent behaviors in children—dependence on someone else to give you a topic, dependence on a story frame to help you plan the writing, dependence on a time frame that's been arbitrarily set, dependence on a standard routine for revision and editing, dependence on a score to tell you whether the writing worked or not—how significant it is that a book comes to us now and asks us to look closely at *in*dependence in the teaching of writing. How significant that someone has finally taken what is perhaps the truest of the truths about writing—that it is a supreme act of independence—and brought it to the classroom.

I can hardly wait to have other teachers of writing read this book. I can hardly wait to get involved in new conversations about independence in the writing workshop. Who knows where they might lead us? Many thanks to Colleen for writing a book that will take us somewhere new.

K. W. R.

Acknowledgments

Though this book is about independence in writing, I wrote it very much depending on others.

My thanks goes, first of all, to my fourth-grade students, past and present. Although time in this book has been compressed in order to tell the story of one year in the life of a classroom, the students described represent four years of students working in an independent workshop and three years of experimentation before that. Every last student has been generous with his or her time, humor, and patience. I appreciate their brave willingness to share their work and stories in this book. I must also thank their families for their understanding and for enduring my constant requests for information and consent forms. Their support and kind words helped me to continue this work.

I am grateful to the entire staff and faculty of P.S. 321. The custodial staff put up with my staying in the building until late into the night and swept around me. The secretaries helped me with the copy machine, forgave my absentmindedness, and always asked how I was doing. Then there are the extraordinary teachers, whose thoughtful input about the teaching of writing and children's needs and whose willingness to answer my questions was incredibly helpful. Especially, I thank Bonni Suslowitz for the cheerleading, Mike Rogers for listening, Adele Schroeter for being a model of an adult understanding children, Jeanne Jahr for asking good questions, Cory Gillette for trying some of my stranger ideas, Liz Ryan for making me laugh, Melanie Oser for helping me to keep things in perspective, and Terry McNulty for being the ultimate bouncing board.

I also thank Rose Iovine, my colleague and second mother. I have been inspired by her love of children and her passion to do right by them. My heartfelt thanks goes to Jenifer Taets, my former teaching partner, who taught me so much about how children learn and how to respect that learning. Kate Pollock, my teaching-partner-in-crime, was absolutely crucial in experimenting with the ideas in this book. Her innate sense of balance and fairness kept me from getting too far off the track.

I am grateful to Liz Phillips, truly a teacher's principal, who supported me throughout all the phases of this book. Caroline Forlano, master teacher and administrator, helped me to keep going through the rough spots and is a positive force in my life. I thank Beth Handman for never saying "no" to my requests for needed books or supplies, and Richie Goldstein for encouraging me to write this book before I knew I could.

I am deeply indebted to Lucy Calkins and the Teachers College Reading and Writing Project. I was fortunate to have begun my teaching career learning from the great minds at the Project. It was one of Lucy Calkins' keynote addresses that inspired me to connect my own writing life with the lives of my students. Her words continue to inspire and direct my development as a teacher and writer. I also thank Kathleen Tolan, my first staff developer, for teaching me more than I thought my brain could hold. Her brilliance in the teaching of reading and writing overwhelms me. Thanks to Carl Anderson, for believing I could write this book and offering to help me in any way he could. I learned much from him about how to talk to children and more importantly, how to listen. I especially thank Stephanie Parsons, for introducing me to Kate Montgomery and commiserating with me about writing. I am also very grateful for her ability to make me laugh at myself.

I need to thank all the people who were in leadership groups with me at the Project. They offered suggestions, stretched my thinking and often kept me going. In particular, Judy Morehead, Emily Smith, Ted Kessler, Mary Chiarella, Brooke Geller, Patty Tabacchi and Sarah Colmaire gave beyond the call of duty.

It is not possible to adequately thank Isoke Nia, whose ideas are the basis for this book and whose inspiration called me to write it. Her encouragement allowed me to finish it. I will always be grateful for her influence in my life and my teaching. I count her as one of my great mentors in life.

Many thanks to Katie Ray, who suggested I turn an article I wrote for her into a book. Her thoughts about writing and how to teach it to children revolutionized my teaching. During this whole process I have alternately cursed and blessed her name.

I must also thank my Tuesday night writing workshop and all its members, past and present. They read from the earliest to latest drafts, giving insights that only writers and non-teachers would be able to offer. I am particularly grateful to Penny Arcade, Elin Ewald, Aaron Hicklin, Jenny Pollack, Leslie Ross, Robin Swid, Brenna Tinkel, and Dave Varing for their humor and patience. And I greatly appreciate Jennifer Belle's countless assists in bringing this book to life and catching my major writer's life faux pas.

I need to thank my personal "Max Perkins," Kate Montgomery, my editor at Heinemann. I am grateful to her for amazing ideas, the surgical precision of her suggestions, and her complete faith. The best parts of this book come from her influence. I'd also like to thank the other folks who helped put this book together, especially Elizabeth Valway and Steve Bernier at Heinemann, Suzanne Heiser, Kim Arney Mulcahy, and Denise Botelho.

I particularly appreciate the primary photographer for this book, Angela Jimenez. Her beautiful photographs capture the students' energy and personality. She was endlessly patient with my writing schedule and my lack of photographic know-how. Without her work there would have only been my amateurish photography to work with.

I am grateful to my friends who supported me, took me out, and listening to me through this whole process. Joslyn Aubin and Tina Encarnacion often lured me away from the city for much needed rest. Sheila Frayne, Margarette Adams and Perry Fisher for whisking me away to Pennsylvania, Coney Island, and for a meal, and wouldn't take no for an answer. Thanks to Kim Kelly, Lisa Shaw, Rachel Einziger, and Mardi Jaskot for celebrating with me and sharing the love of teaching. I appreciate Jan Valle's unconditional belief in my teaching and eternally positive outlook on life. I am grateful to Eva Berbegal and Connie Lynn for their expressions of confidence. And I thank Kate Roberts, for being a good friend and an inspiration.

I need to thank my own writing teachers for instilling in me a love and awe of words: Susan Weurer (my seventh-grade teacher), Ted Kopacki (my high school teacher) and Perry Glasser (my college professor). I also want to express my appreciation to my earliest teachers of teaching: Karen Siegel, Paula Sable, Fran Schoonmaker, and Marjorie Seigel.

My deepest thanks goes to my family. I am grateful to my mother, Joan Cruz, for loving me and supporting my love of teaching and writing; my father, Wil Cruz, an educator, for believing me into a person who persists; my brother, Mike Cruz for complete understanding. I also need to thank the Baldasare clan for their love, support and enthusiasm during this whole process.

Finally, the person who most deserves my gratitude is my partner, Nadine Baldasare. She read countless versions of this book, taught me much about the ways different minds work, and provided technical assistance. Even more note-worthy was her seemingly never-ending patience while I spent countless hours lost at my desk and in a grouchy mood. Thank you.

Introduction

Beginning when I was about nine years old, until I was thirteen, I would slip into the back room of our house whenever I had a chance. It was the kind of room with a door that stuck when it rained and you had to push with your shoulder to get it open. It was filled with piles of magazines, boxes of books, and dusty sporting equipment. But its treasure was in the far corner underneath the window with the drooping Venetian blinds.

My father's beige IBM electric typewriter.

I would sit in the big orange vinyl chair and roll up to the metal cart the typewriter sat on. When I flipped the big black switch to turn it on, the typewriter rumbled to life, vibrating and humming like a car. I loved the satisfaction of the clicking keys as I pecked away my summer vacations and weekends. I was convinced I would be the next S. E. Hinton, with a novel published by the time I was sixteen. I knew all it would take was time and dedication for my launch to literary superstardom to be assured.

Even though I didn't know it then, I was definitely living as a writer. Writing was not a subject I was taught in school every day. I was lucky if it was taught once a week. Yet, I was a reader and a lover of words and I knew I wanted to write books one day. The way I figured it, the only way I was going to write a book was by taking matters into my own hands.

I developed that love of writing as I grew older. I majored in writing in college. I joined writing groups. I wrote short stories and worked on a novel. I still struggled to identify myself as a writer, but I remained in love with the act of writing. I loved to create characters, build worlds for them to inhabit, and play the role of creator.

When I became a teacher, I held fast to that child who slid into the orange chair with the cracked vinyl seat. I knew not every student I taught would be as enamored with words and writing as I was. A lot of children would probably rather be doing anything than sitting alone in a room with only stories for company.

Other children would never have a back room with a hidden typewriter, or even a spare notebook lying around if they did want to write. Many children would not know how to live a writing life without the support of school.

I wondered what would happen if the mystery was taken out of writing. I wondered what would happen if students were told why they were being taught certain things about writing, like how a writer makes writing decisions or why punctuation mattered. I wondered what would happen if they were taught something I had instinctively known as a child—they could make or write anything they wanted.

As a fourth-grade teacher at P.S. 321 in Brooklyn, New York, I have had opportunities to teach with those ideas in mind. My colleagues are incredibly gifted and dedicated, as is my supportive administration. I have also been lucky to have been involved with rich staff development opportunities from the Teachers College Reading and Writing Project. All of these combined have helped me to focus my efforts over the past several years on the study of literacy, in particular the study of writing.

Like all good teaching practices, there came a time when I felt that my teaching of writing needed to be looked at. I knew that I was doing a decent job of teaching my students the nuts and bolts of writing as well as exposing them to a variety of genres and writing techniques that were more advanced. But something nagged at me. I felt that my efforts to create tight, rigorous units of study that challenged my students while preparing them for the new standards they would be tested on, I was losing sight of something. I was losing sight of the independent girl I once was, alone in a room with just a typewriter and a story to tell. I knew I wanted to give that experience to my students as much as I wanted to expose them to the other aspects of writing.

Then I heard Isoke Nia, then staff developer for the Teachers College Reading and Writing project, speak about helping students build a sense of independence in their writing, and I joined her leadership group in order to study that idea further. I then began my own study of this idea of independence in the writing workshop. I read *Coping with Chaos* by Brian Cambourne and Jan Turnbill and discovered the level of independence kindergartners were able to achieve. It seemed far beyond what I had been expecting from my nine- and ten-year-olds. I read books written for the students themselves, like Ralph Fletcher's *How Writers Work* and *Live Writing*. I listened to Katie Ray speak at a summer institute about how children can learn to read like writers and become capable of raising the level of their work while achieving a certain degree of independence.

Along the way, by learning from my mentors, my colleagues, and my students, I realized that children needed to learn to become independent as much as they needed to learn the fundamentals of writing.

By becoming independent they would be able to own their development as a writer. By becoming independent they would be able to demystify the act of writing. By becoming independent they would be able to chart their own course through their writing lives and see how writing plays a role in people's lives outside the confines of the classroom.

And, as an early reader of this book pointed out, if we can teach students to become independent, there will come a time when there is no longer a distinction between being an "independent" writer and being a writer. Once the child is all grown up, she or he has simply become a writer.

This book is about my and my students' journey as learners. It follows my discoveries as I tried to improve and refine my teaching of writing. It focuses on one year and how independence in the writing workshop affected and colored different aspects of the classroom and the students in that year.

While the book's content is mostly in chronological order, it is also divided into topics I felt were the most affected by independence: the beginning of the year, the use of mentors in the workshop, the writer's notebook, the community, troubles that were uncovered, and assessment. I know when I read professional books I am frequently tweaking them to fit the students who are sitting in my classroom that year, and I expect the same to be true for this book.

I suspect the subject of building students' independence will become a lifelong study for me. With this book I simply tried to tell the story of my experiences, the successes and failures, of trying to teach my students to create and lead their own writing lives outside of my classroom. I hope you find it useful.

Independent
Writing

1
Getting Started

"This year is going to be different than any other year," I said as I looked at their thirty-two freshly scrubbed faces. It was the one day of the year, besides picture day, when I knew every student would be dressed in a carefully chosen outfit with neatly coiffed hair.

"This year we are going to write about our passions. The things we love the most in the world. We will write about horses, baby sisters, pizza with extra cheese, video games and the New York Liberty Basketball Team," I continued.

They exchanged looks. Even though it was the first day of school, they still needed to make that connection with their fellow classmates. *This lady is crazy.*

"We're going to make stuff. We'll make cookbooks, posters, plays, and newspapers," I said. A few kids started to smile. "We're going to write more this year than you have in your entire life," I added in a conspiratorial voice. The silence was broken by a few groans mixed with a few cheers.

"You are going to be able to write *anything you want!*" I gushed, ignoring some of the now louder moans.

A fair-skinned girl with brown hair and freckles, who I would later learn was named Nili, raised her hand and asked, "We can make anything we want? Even comic books?"

"Yes. Even though I would have to admit that comic books are just about the hardest thing a person can ever try to write all by him or herself. But if you're brave enough, and you really love comic books, then I suppose you can," I said.

They stayed silent. They alternated between staring at me and staring at each other.

"This year we're going to learn how to write and publish our own pieces independently—without having to get a teacher's help every time you want to write something," I said. I waited for the idea to sink in and the next inevitable question to come. It did.

"Are we going to start that now?" asked a quiet African American girl with bouncy curls who I would later learn was named Kenya.

I shook my head and smiled, "Not right now, no. We have a few other things we have to do first—like get to know each other. We also need to get used to being in a writing workshop again, learn a few things that are going to be new this year, that sort of thing. But, in a few weeks we will be ready to learn how to write independently."

My students were going to learn how to become independent writers within the writing workshop. They would develop and realize their own ideas for writing projects. Those projects, of their own design, would be worked on inside and outside of the classroom while they concurrently worked on the planned class curriculum. In that way, I hoped students would see the role writing played outside of the classroom and inside their lives.

Can Children Write Independently?

Although I didn't realize it for some time, the ideas I introduced to my students that first day of school were ideas I had been playing with for awhile.

Since I first entered the classroom I have taught writing in the "writing workshop" model I learned through Lucy Calkins' work and the work of the Reading and Writing Project at Teachers College, Columbia University. The model espouses teaching students the process of writing by guiding them through gathering ideas and thoughts in writers' notebooks, all the way through drafting, revising, and creating well-crafted finished pieces. Over the years, as I continued to study this model I learned how to confer with my students, create units of study, and help my students to master writing conventions along the way.

For several years my typical writing lesson was fairly predictable. I would teach a mini-lesson. That mini-lesson would be one of a string of mini-lessons that fit into a subject we were currently studying as a whole class, which when put all together would be a unit of study. During a unit of study about feature articles, for example, I might teach a lesson on how to use quotes from experts. Students would then take the lesson and use it during the work period. A student might find places in her draft where expert quotes would create a richer article.

While the students worked I would circulate through the room meeting with individual students offering one-on-one support and teaching, also called conferring. After the students worked for a chunk of time, and I had met with as many as I could, we would gather up again. The last few minutes of the period would be used to share how their work went that day and to teach into anything I had noticed during the work time.

The next day would go much the same. I would teach another lesson connected to the one before, and students would go off to work. If a student finished the work that had been assigned during that day's lesson she could go back and write in her writer's notebook until the class had caught up with her. All of the writing produced by students in my class was connected to the unit of study we were working on.

I was moderately pleased with the writing workshop that was up and running in my classroom. Students produced a lot of writing in the course of a year and the quality of writing was high. When I looked through students' pieces I could clearly see each lesson I taught during each study. But something nagged at me. I knew that students had made daily reading a part of their lives. I knew that students understood their reading habits, what kinds of books they liked, what magazines they gravitated to, and the like. I wasn't so sure they had the same sense of how writing fit into their daily life outside of school. They were writing well, but was I helping them to become lifelong writers the way I knew I helped them to become lifelong readers?

I doubted it.

Of course I knew there would be *some* students from my class who would be able to see ways to fit writing into their lives, maybe even become writers when they grew up. I also knew that a majority of my students learned how to write solid pieces in a variety of genres; however, few of them saw how writing could become a lifelong habit. They could not see how writing would fit into the life of a firefighter, lawyer, or plumber.

When I looked at myself as a writer I knew there were things I learned and people who supported me that had helped to develop the habits that supported my love of writing. I needed to look at my writing life and compare it to the writing life I offered my students in order to see where I was falling short of my goal to create lifelong writers.

First of all, I knew my students produced good quality pieces because I was there to support them every step of the way. They knew what pieces to write and when to write them because I set the writing curriculum and expectations for them. I tried to make sure the things I taught were lifetime skills so that my students could apply their writing knowledge into any piece they created. But I was very aware that I was not teaching my students how to envision good quality pieces outside of my classroom.

Secondly, I knew that my students' writing identity was very wrapped up in school. After all, despite all my talking about ways they could take writing into the world, they rarely seemed to do so. They didn't seem to be making the connection, despite what I told them or the kinds of writing we did in class, that writers wrote for so many reasons. Reasons such as communicating to other people, entertainment, expressing feelings, convincing people of ideas, and others were lost on them. They wrote to please me, their classmates, even their families, but rarely did they write to please themselves.

I was also not happy with management of my writing workshop. Too often I felt that students were wasting time as they waited for the rest of the class to catch up with them in their work. I worried that not all my students were having their writing needs met. What happened to the student who loved science fiction but never had a chance to write it? What about the struggling students who would do better if they could spend time mastering one genre rather than constantly leaping from one to the other?

I was in this funk of writing workshop dissatisfaction when I first heard Isoke Nia, then director of research and a staff developer at the Reading and Writing Project, speak about "Independence in the Writing Workshop." I had heard Isoke speak on a variety of topics over the years, from genre studies to curriculum design, and was always moved to be a better teacher through her words. But when she talked about students' need to create independent writing lives and how we should teach them how, I was flabbergasted. She was speaking to exactly what I had questioned.

I thought it exciting, but frightening. I wondered how students could publish anything of quality without me teaching them everything they needed to know about the piece. I wondered how my struggling students could publish independently when they were barely able to finish the pieces I asked for.

My biggest worry was management. I wondered how I could possibly balance teaching my own curriculum with teaching thirty-two individual projects as well— a terrifying concept.

Then I realized I didn't need to teach every single genre, crafting technique, or structure. I could use writers to do that.

The idea of published writers as mentors had excited me since the first day I heard Katie Ray, the acclaimed writing researcher and staff developer, speak. Katie talked about how adult writers regularly studied the work of other writers in order to raise the level of their work. She said it made sense for us to teach our students how to do this as well. We could teach our students to study published writers and the techniques those writers used as a way to raise the level of the students' work. Some teachers call those writers that students studied "mentor authors."

In past years, after I introduced the concept of mentor authors to my class, their level of writing improved dramatically. I knew in theory it should apply to any writing work the students did, that this skill should be one they could carry out of school and use into adulthood. If kids wanted to write something, anything, all kids needed to do was study other writers who wrote the sort of thing they wanted to write, or in a style the kids admired, and—voila! I just didn't know yet how to help my students make this connect to work outside of what their teacher wanted from them.

I knew there were other people my students could rely on for help—the writers in my classroom, their own colleagues. They could act as writers do in an adult writer's workshop. They could critique, support, offer resources and that all-important sense of community that the isolated world of writing sometimes lacks. I had not had much success getting my students to be good partners in writing for each other. But I also knew that I had not spent much time in my classroom focusing on this skill—and a skill it was. I knew I was good at criticizing other writers' work, and also knew that it was a learned skill and therefore something I could teach my students.

Finally, my students could find support in themselves as writers. They could nurture themselves, stretch their own ideas, and record their plans and thoughts. I felt the best place for a writer's self-support is the writer's notebook, where my students worked well. But I could never have predicted the revolution that would occur once my students began publishing independently, transforming their notebooks. These notebooks, the guts of their writing lives, would prove instrumental in their journey as independent writers.

By the time I had finished my first experimental work in guiding my students towards writing independently, I had come to a firm conclusion: independence in the writing workshop is one of the most valuable skills we can teach our students. Every healthy writing workshop allows young writers opportunities to choose topics, develop their craft, learn from peers, and master conventions. When students learn how to create and navigate their own writing lives through independent work they are able to take the gifts of the workshop model even further. The students then have the tools to explore their passions, decide on their audience, design their own writing plans, and set their own pace. They are more able to become lifelong writers because it is their vision they are following.

Also, what had worried me most—that most struggling students would not be able to do the work—turned out to be a needless fear. In fact, once my students began writing independently, even my most reluctant writers raced to get started. Writing had developed a real life value for them. What I found most amazing was that these struggling students often excelled at writing and reveled in the act of writing once they *owned* it. Writing became one of the few areas in the school day where they had complete control, and they treasured it.

Envisioning the Curriculum Calendar with Independence in Mind

Just as I taught a unit about fractions in math, and a unit on the U.S. Constitution in social studies, I taught my writing curriculum in units that connected to create my writing curriculum. Knowing that, I needed to think about how every writing unit would have some level of independence in it. I needed to consider which units my students needed experience with before I formally introduced independence. For example, I thought it was very important that students understood how writers lived their lives, so that students developed their own writing lifestyles. It was also important for my students to develop comfort with a writing process early in the year. Literacy expert Ralph Fletcher says there is no single writing process that all writers go through for every writing piece. In *How Writers Work* he writes, "Writing doesn't work that way. Some people need less time to prewrite, more time to rough draft. I believe that the idea of a one-size-fits-all writing process has turned off some talented young writers" (2000, 3). I couldn't agree more. But I also think that naming common steps that writers take as they move through a piece is an essential quality of a good writing workshop because a common language is key when discussing anything. Different communities use different names for the process a writer goes through. The important thing is that every child in our classrooms understands that writers do go through a process when they write and are able to talk about that process.

I knew that in order to truly become a classroom where independence flourished I had to reconsider the typical way I taught a mini-lesson in addition to looking at my units of study. There had to be room for students to make independent choices from the first days in September to the last days in June. Using what I had learned about curriculum design from Isoke Nia and Katie Ray, I designed a curriculum calendar that combined my school's expectations for my grade, New York State standards, and my own goals for my students. In the end, my curriculum calendar looked like Figure 1–1.

Within each unit I planned out my major goals, and some key lessons I knew I would teach no matter what, as well as the assessments I would use. I also made sure that woven through each unit I taught there was a thread of independence. At first this was a bit of a challenge until I worked out a series of questions I kept in mind whenever I planned out a unit.

- *What are my baseline to loftiest expectations for my students in this unit?* There were certain basics that I expected every child to master in a unit. There were other concepts that I wanted everyone to be exposed to, but I did not necessarily expect everyone to be ready for. It was helpful for me to be clear about what realistic expectations were for each unit.
- *Which past lessons do I want to include this time?* While it is true I needed to tailor my teaching to the students who sat in front of me, there were lessons that I knew I needed or wanted to teach every year. Kathleen Tolan, staff developer for the Teachers College Reading and Writing Project, taught me how important it is for teachers to write out plans from good lessons already taught. There is no reason to create a brand-new lesson when a solid one already exists.
- *How will I assess? How will this assessment build on my previous assessments? How will assessment guide my students and me in present and future projects?* I

		4-305'S WRITING CURRICULUM CALENDAR	
Length of Study	**Unit of Study**	**Genre of Finished Piece**	**Ways Unit Supports Independence**
Two days	Assessment	Any genre	Gives quick basic knowledge of students' strengths, weaknesses, and attitudes toward writing.
4 weeks	Writerly Life	Any genre	Students develop sense of selves as writers: • Preferred genres • Ideal writing situation • Favorite topics • How they move through process
9 days	Punctuation	Any genre	Students learn about punctuation: • Students study the role punctuation plays with regards to clarity of ideas and ease for their readers. • Students are able to move more quickly and independently through the process because they are not caught on simple punctuation snafus.
2 weeks	Independence	Any genre	*Students formally begin independent writing lives.*
3 weeks	Choosing a Mentor	Any genre	Students begin to master choice and use of mentors independently, which fosters their: • Ability to try any mentor-modeled genre without teacher support; • Ability to study structures of texts to revise own work alone if needed; • Ability to look at parts of texts (beginning, ending, dramatic scene, etc.) and independently apply mentors' moves to own work; • Ability to use mentor to problem solve or improve writing. *Students continue to work on independent projects concurrently.*

Figure 1–1 My Writing Curriculum Calendar (Adapted from Isoke Nia's work)

Length of Study	Unit of Study	Genre of Finished Piece	Ways Unit Supports Independence
5 weeks	Nonfiction: feature article	Feature article	Students learn skills that apply to a variety of nonfiction writing options that students might want to explore independently. These skills include: • Ways to research secondary resources • Interviews • Surveys • Observations • Organization of facts • Planning for pieces with subheads *Students continue to work on independent projects concurrently.*
4 weeks	The ELA Test	The ELA Test	Students learn test-taking skills that can be applied in test-taking situations throughout life. Excellent opportunity for students to strengthen ability to balance two writing focuses. *Students continue to work on independent projects concurrently.*
7 weeks	Realistic Fiction	Realistic Fiction short story and/or picture book	Students learn skills that apply to a variety of fiction-writing options that students might want to explore independently. These skills include: • Character creation • Building a believable plot • Subtle and obvious ways to move time • Description of setting • Use of dialogue • Creating suspense and building tension • Titling a piece • Knowing when to write in scenes or summarize *Students continue to work on independent projects concurrently.*

Figure 1–1 Continued

Length of Study	Unit of Study	Genre of Finished Piece	Ways Unit Supports Independence
1 week	Independence (revisited)	Any genre	Students hone independent writing skills, trouble-shoot and reassess plans. *Students will work on independent projects.*
3 weeks	Poetry	Poetry anthology (at least 5 poems)	Students learn skills to help them improve the quality of their poetry and poetic language, which might be used while independently writing poetry in its various forms. *Students continue to work on independent projects concurrently.*
8 days	Revision	Any genre as long as piece was prev. published in class	Students study and practice several revision techniques and the reasons writers use them. Most students will leave study with a handful of strategies that work well for them and their independent writing style. *Students continue to work on independent projects concurrently.*
6 weeks	Photojournalism	Photo Essay	Students learn about the connection between pictures and text. For students with more connection to visual storytelling this offers another option to build upon in their independent work. *Students continue to work on independent projects concurrently. Students make plans for summer and future independent writing projects*

Figure 1–1 Continued

used my baseline goals to establish what I planned to assess. I also found it helpful to create my assessments early in my planning so that I was sure that what I taught was aligned with the assessment. While I assessed in a variety of ways, I did make sure to use at least one self-assessment form per unit. Those self-assessment forms served as guides for students when they were in the final stages of a piece, as a form of communicating my expectations to parents, and as a means of opening a dialogue with my students about their work. It was also interesting to watch how the assessments changed and expanded as the year moved on and the expectations of what had been mastered were added to. (See Figures 1–2 and 1–3.)

Punctuation Study
. , ; : ! ? . . . ( ) –

Name: _____   Date: _____

☑ My piece has an attractive cover with the title of my piece, my name and the date.

☑ My piece is typed or written in pen in my neatest handwriting.

☑ I chose to (circle one): –revise and re-publish a piece I already published

        – re-work and publish an entry from my notebook

        – go through all the steps of the process and publish a brand new piece

☑ This checklist is attached to my piece.

☑ Any drafts of my piece are attached to my piece.

☑ I checked my piece for correct spelling.

☑ I had an adult read over my piece to offer suggestions, check my spelling, punctuation and grammar.

☑ I am proud of my piece! (I've published twice this year already.)

Check off the kinds of punctuation you used in your piece:

☑ Period

☑ Exclamation Point

☑ Question Mark

☐ Ellipses

☐ Dash

☑ Parentheses

☑ Comma

☑ (drum roll please . . .) Semi-colon

Figure 1–2 A Checklist for Our Punctuation Study

Author: _____ Mentor: _____
Title: **Megan Makes a new friend**
☐ I wrote in the form of a short story
☐ I wrote in the form of a picture book
☑ I wrote in the form of (describe): **a long form**

My Realistic Fiction Assessment Sheet

Use this sheet to help guide you for your published piece. After you have checked to see that you have done each thing on the list, give yourself a rubric score: 1=below standards ; 2=almost at standards ; 3=meeting standards ; 4=way above standards . Don't fill out the column "Colleen's Score". I'll fill that in when I read your piece with <u>this sheet attached</u>.

*Don't forget – these are all things we will have learned by the time this piece is due

What's In the Piece?	Score I gave myself	Colleen's Score
The Usual Suspects	4	---
I used punctuation well.	4	
I used good grammar.	3	
I capitalized correctly.	4	
I used paragraphs well.	4	
It was typed or written in pen, neatly.	4	
It has a cover and "about the author".	3	
Character Development	3	---
I tried a lot of ways to create a character in my WNB (9 elements).	3	
I knew my character's past (childhood, family, etc.)	4	

Figure 1–3 Months Later, the Checklist Has Been Replaced by a Rubic

- *What choices will I offer my students while working through this unit?* While students always had a choice of topics in my classroom, I tried to make sure there were other opportunities for choice as well. I expected students to try most things I taught them at least once, though, whether or not they chose to add a particular strategy or skill to their repertoire was left up to

I talked to other writers about my character.	3	
I planned a plot using my character's issue.	3	
My character seemed "real".	4	
My character had inner thoughts.	4	
My character CHANGED!	3	
My character had wants/needs.	3	
My character had relationships with others.	4	
Plot Development	3	---
My plot was centered on one event.	4	
My plot had TROUBLE.	4	
My plot was connected to my character's issue.	4	
There was a clear beginning, middle and end.	3	
My plot had a *resolution*.	3	
Setting	4	---
My story had a setting.	4	
I described the setting well.	4	
There was a connection between my character and the setting.	3	
Time	4	---
Time passed in my story.	4	
The time made sense with my plot.	3	
I used obvious ways to show time passed.	3	
I used subtle ways to show time passed.	4	

Figure 1–3 Continued

them. For example, if I my goal was to teach students to be planful writers I taught a mini-lesson on "Writers Make Plans." Then I introduced a variety of planning methods: outlines, flow charts, diagrams, and storyboards. While I expected all my students to plan, the choice of technique was up to them.

Craft	-4	---
My piece had a strong sense of voice.	4	
I chose a perspective that made my piece stronger (first, second or third person)	4	
I used dialogue well.	4	
My piece had a dramatic scene.	3	
My lead was strong.	3'	
I used fresh language.	4	
The title of my piece was well thought out.	4	
I knew when to stretch a moment or shrink it.	4	
I used my mentor well.	4	
I ended well. I didn't "drop a cow".	4	
EXTRAS-you are not need to do these . . . but if you did -	---	---
I used flashback.	4	
I wrote a prologue, epilogue or both.	3/4	
I had a subplot.		
I used a "fringe technique" when developing my character.	4	
I did something else special. I ...	used the way Megan says "like a lot in it.	

Any Comments? What you think you did well? What you plan on doing differently next time? Questions?

What if you don't finished by May 2 I will plan to use good dialogue next time I revised really well.

Figure 1–3 Continued

- *How will I differentiate instruction so that all students will be able to work as independently as possible? What, if anything, will I need to modify?* As a general education teacher, and later a co-teacher in an inclusive setting, I found it increasingly important to keep in mind that my students were a heterogeneous group. While I did not believe that my overarching goals should change for any of my students (we were all going to learn the basics of feature article writing no matter what), the approach that I used did vary. Ultimately, my aim was to ensure that the goals were achievable with as much independence as possible no matter what the student's capabilities.

While there are other questions I might have asked myself that were specific to a particular unit in writing, I have used this list regularly while planning everything from a revision study to test prep. Of course, the way I planned my curriculum calendar, units, and mini-lessons was not the only thing that changed once I made the decision to make my classroom a place where independence thrived. In the years since I began studying and teaching independence in the writing workshop, I realized that my students, my physical classroom, every subject I taught, and even I have been influenced by it. Independence and its influences permeated everything.

Laying the Foundations for a Writing Unit of Study in Independence

Step One: Laying Out the Supplies

I set up my classroom to support independent writers even before I met my new students. I thought about my own writing life as I planned what to include as tools and resources. I wanted my students' experience to be as authentic as possible. I thought about what I used every time I wrote. What books? What materials? Whatever I found necessary or merely helpful should be there for my students to use as well. I knew when I wrote anything from a letter to my class's families to an article for a journal there were certain supplies I found indispensable. I always had a jar full of pens and pencils within reach so if I lost the one I was working with I did not need to slow my pace. I used sticky notes and highlighters almost daily to mark important places in texts I referred to and to jot notes to myself. I had a good thesaurus on hand for when the right word was not quick in coming. I had my trusty *Elements of Style* by Strunk and White to thwart my grammatical foibles. It was important for me to remember that in my own writing life I frequently relied on tools, and my students should have the same advantages.

After much thought I placed a bookcase in the front of the classroom (painted silver for dramatic effect) that contained almost everything a writer might need. (See Figure 1–4.) Each year I have tinkered a bit with the contents, but the basics have remained the same. Student-supplied writing folders sat in a basket on the top shelf, eventually serving as a sort of writer's filing cabinet for each student. The folders contained:

- students' drafts
- check-off sheets
- assessment forms

Figure 1–4 The writing shelf holds a variety of resources for the student writer.

- copies of texts the whole class shared
- proposal forms.

Next to the folders sat a wire basket where students placed their completely finished pieces.

The next shelves were designed for maximum writing supply independence. There were piles of lined paper and white drawing paper. Extra pens and pencils shared space with a box filled with paper clips and rubber bands. Wicker baskets lined another shelf filled with highlighters, post-its and index cards. Grammar books, thesauruses, books of quotations, and writing exercises leaned into each other. (See list at end of chapter.) On the last shelf sat piles of editing check-off sheets and proposal/self-assessment forms.

When the students walked through the classroom door on the first day of school the "silver shelf," as it came to be called, caught many eyes. After I gave them my talk about what we had planned for the year in writing I let them peruse the shelf, and I explained that in our classroom they did not need to ask for any of the supplies that were on the shelf—they should simply take what they needed as they needed. For many students this was a great departure from previous classroom experiences where paper might be stored in a closet that only the teacher or a monitor had access to. Other students were used to keeping all of their own writing supplies in their desks. Still other students were used to the supplies being accessible; but the idea of an area where all the supplies for writing were in a central location was new. We discussed the importance of being able to have access to supplies when they were needed, but to be aware that everyone needed to share supplies so we also needed to be conscientious in our use. We also talked about the community aspect of supply sharing so that students understood the responsibility they had to each other, even when they were being independent-minded.

I intentionally did not discuss the smaller details of what was on the silver shelf, such as the proposal sheets. We would have time to get to that later when I formally introduced independent writing to them. Instead we moved into our September writing curriculum, which began with me getting to know the students better as writers.

Step Two: Getting to Know the Students Through Assessment

Since I had deliberately introduced our upcoming independent work on the first day of school to whet their appetites, I knew the kids would be on the lookout for the first signs that "this year would be different." But first I needed to get to know them as soon as possible.

There are many ways to quickly assess our students' writing in the first few days of school. Some teachers have students create a fully fleshed-out piece in a few in-class writing sessions with little or no teacher intervention in order to best observe the students' work styles and prior writing knowledge. Other teachers have students fill out questionnaires about writing in order to get a quick sense of students' perceptions of writing, as well as a general sense of writing mechanics. Since my focus was understanding the kind of teaching I would need to do in order to build independence, I wanted to know if the students could write well-organized pieces and to learn their perception of themselves as writers. I asked them during one writing period to write as much as they could about the kind of writer they were. "You might want to talk about what you really like about writing, what you hate about it. You might want to talk about the kind of writing you think you're best at. What helps you to do the best kind of writing you can do?" I said.

From watching the way they held their bodies as they wrote, their level of tension, and by reading their self-assessments I was able to get a pretty good idea of the make-up of writers we had in the class. (See Figures 1–5 and 1–6.)

Figure 1–5 The beginning writing assessment taught me a lot about these students' attitudes towards writing.

During the first month I also, as we moved through the paces of our first unit of study, watched for a handful of things which contributed to what I like to think of as "independence readiness."

- *Student has understanding that writing is a process.* The student does not need to know the vocabulary for the writing process in September. She or he should understand that there are several steps to creating a finished piece.
- *Student has memory of writing success.* A lot of students remember a good school writing experience. Some students however, must be guided to remember at least one positive writing experience: making a card for a neighbor, writing a song with a friend, and so on. This positive memory may be referred to when independent writing gets tough.
- *Student reflects on his/her writing.* Some students are more self-aware than others. For many writers, adults as well as children, knowing whether a piece is good or not is difficult. But all of our writers should be able to talk a little about what was hard, what went well, and what they would like to improve on.
- *Student has interests or passions that can be used to create writing pieces.* Again, most students walk in our door with lots of strong feelings. Some students can list their loves, hates, and fascinations without hesitation. Other students need to be guided a little to uncover those things—especially since they might have been told those things were not valued in school.

I'm the kind of writer who loves writing but is sometimes unsure of my work. I'm the kind of writer who really likes to express my ideas about the writing I do. I really like to write survival stories. Also I like to write a little non-fiction, I also like to write about exciting memories, and funny stories. I sometimes put to many ideas in one story and instead of 5 pages it becomes 12 pages. I sometimes can't think of anything to write about but I solve it by making lists about what I like, and I have so many Ideas burst into my mind I have to eliminate good ones. I love when I have a really good idea because I get so into it I'm unaware of what's going on around me. Then if someone interrupts, I lose the good felling I had is gone. I really like making

Figure 1–6 The beginning writing assessment taught me a lot about these students' attitudes towards writing.

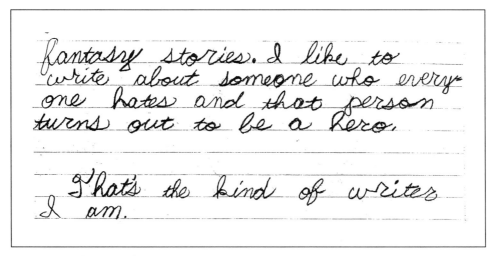

Fantasy stories. I like to write about someone who everyone hates and that person turns out to be a hero.

That's the kind of writer I am.

Figure 1–6 Continued

While I informally kept track of these things in my conference notes, it might be a good idea to keep a checklist for each child. Then, when it's time to plan for the unit on independence, it's easy enough to lay out all the notes and checklists to make a thumbnail sketch of what kinds of lessons might still need to be taught.

Nili was the kind of girl who loved to make her teachers happy, and a solid, if insecure, writer who asked "is this right?" at least once during a writing period. She wrote in her neatest handwriting in her writer's notebook, and she decorated each of her finished pieces with painstaking care. I hoped that by the end of the year she would be able to trust herself to finish pieces without needing my constant approval. Aidan was a spirited kid with a fabulous sense of humor. He was proud of his Irish-Jewish heritage and talked about it often. He loved sports and singing more than he loved the inside of the classroom, probably because those things came easy to him, whereas academic work required more effort. My goal for Aidan was for him to find something in writing that would hold his attention enough to make it worth the effort.

Ruthie was as quietly proud of her writing as she was of all her schoolwork. She took a special pride in her poetry and had already written several poems over the summer vacation. She liked to sketch drawings of herself with her curly brown hair flying everywhere. Since she was such a strong student, her biggest hurdle seemed to be getting her to talk more about her successes so that others could learn from her example. I hoped she would take that on.

Oscar was probably my most struggling student academically. He had a number of services including speech and occupational therapy. He had a difficult time forming letters with his pencil, let alone putting together sentences. "I hate writing!" he wrote at the beginning of the year. Whenever it was writing time I knew we would have some behavioral issues. I wanted Oscar to find topics that were important enough to him to share with other people through writing and to be willing to do the work in order to make that happen. Oscar was proud of his Puerto Rican background and often told stories connected to his family and his visits to Puerto Rico. I wondered if those stories would be the key to writing, or if something else would be. Kenya was an academically stronger student than Oscar, especially when it came to reading, which she loved. She also adored writing in her writer's notebook, although I later discovered it read more like a diary. Kenya had a difficult time with spelling and capitalization, however. She would get so frustrated with her inability to make things look "right" that she would throw up her arms and abandon her plans for more complex pieces. My goal was for her to let loose a little so that she could say what she wanted to say first, then master the art of the final edit.

Then there was blond-haired, blue-eyed Aaron, who was somewhat introverted with peers but very talkative during lessons. He was in many ways my biggest challenge. He had a complex vocabulary and was an avid reader, but when it came to writing he tended to write simplistic pieces with predictable language that he grudgingly produced. He seemed to believe he knew everything I had to teach him even before he began fourth grade. My biggest battle with him in the beginning of the year was his proclamation, "But, I'm done," as a response to revision conferences. He of course carried the burden of one of my loftiest goals—I wanted his skill in writing to be matched by his love of it.

Those six students were just a sampling of my class. Each was distinctive, with his or her own interests, talents, and struggles. It was precisely because of that variety, the same variety teachers see every year, that I knew teaching them to live independent writing lives would be invaluable to them. After all, I knew I would not be able to meet all their writing needs by myself, but I could teach them how to meet their own needs, as well as their goals.

Step Three: Studying the Writerly Life

Many teachers who hold classroom writing workshops begin the year by looking closely at how a writer lives, and guiding students to live their own versions of a life as a writer. Lucy Calkins refers to this in her book *The Art of Teaching Writing* as "living the writerly life."

In the unit on writerly life, my students have the opportunity to be guided step by step through the writing process. They study how writers live their lives while learning about what works best for their writing lives. They navigate the writing process being taught by their teacher, while beginning to customize their own process. By the end of the unit they complete their first writing piece of the year to gain a sense of what it is like to see a writing piece through to the end.

I typically begin this unit by talking about myself as a writer. I talk about where I like to write, what my writing space looks like, what tools I like to use. I show my writer's notebook and my fancy writing pen. I talk about what makes me eager to write. I talk about that tingle in my toes when I get a good idea and how excited I am when I get to start a brand new notebook. I talk about how proud of myself I am when I finish a project and get to show it to my friends.

Teachers I know who are less comfortable with identifying themselves as writers have tried a couple of different ways to model the "writerly life." They sometimes focus on less literary forms of writing such as letters to old friends, wedding speeches, or lesson plans. They talk about the practicality of writing and how good it feels to see writing serve a purpose. This may even be a better model than my own because the chances are pretty good that some students can identify more with this type of writing life.

Other teachers choose a favorite writer or two who have talked a lot about the writing life. For example, Jacqueline Woodson writes about her work and has a kid-friendly website that offers details about the process she went through for several of her books.

No matter how students learn about it, students should understand that writers live in ways that help them be productive, give them ideas for future pieces, and hone their craft. Learning about how writers live is important for any writing workshop, but it is doubly so when we expect our students to mold an independent writing life outside the classroom. They need to see how people who live their whole lives as writers balance creativity and practicality, without teachers to answer to.

I also like to use those first weeks of school for the storytelling, writing exercises, community building, and books that inspire writing, giving students as much time as possible to build their writer-selves. Those writer-selves will be cultivated throughout the year as they learn to become more and more independent. They discover what is comfortable for them in terms of pace and proximity of other students, and even whether they prefer to write in pen so they are not tempted to erase fragile ideas from their notebooks. I also encourage them to explore forms and genres that they feel drawn to.

Oscar, with his love of hip-hop's rhythms and his hatred for writing long pieces, was inclined to work on poetry throughout the unit. He combined our explorations of our lives and memories to create a poetic version of the old "What I did for summer vacation" chestnut. Ruthie felt like she wanted to try a genre that she loved to read but had never written in. She combined what she had learned about immigration in third grade with her desire to write historical fiction to create a short story for her first piece. These initial published pieces were my first peek into my students' writer-selves and a preview of the independent work to come. I made sure to pay close attention as they moved through the process.

Through it all, I thought of things I should do in the unit to help pave the way for the independent work to come. I used the following "to do" list to make sure that the threads of independence were evident even in those early weeks :

- *Offer Choices During Mini-lessons.* Whenever possible I tried to ensure that students had at least one choice to make per mini-lesson. For example, if we were creating a timeline of our writing life I gave students the choice of using words, pictures, symbols, or a combination. Those small choices help slowly transition students into larger choices later, such as pacing and deadlines.
- *Enforce Supply Responsibility.* Students learned early on that if they needed anything (a pencil, paper, or an eraser, for example) they needed to be responsible for retrieving it during the appropriate times in our classroom.
- *Create Editing and Assignment Checklists.* By taking some time before each study and deciding what I wanted my students to do, I enabled them to independently monitor their own work. I offered checklists dedicated purely to standard writing conventions as well as checklists that enumerated my expectations for each published piece.
- *Introduce the Writing Process Chart.* I showed the students the writing process chart many teachers have in their rooms. The one in my room broke steps of the writing process into six smaller chunks. Students were able to move a magnet with their name on it as they navigated the steps. This allowed students to mark their process graphically and also made them accountable for their progression.

There are a variety of wonderful resources that help explain the workshop structure, the writer's notebook, and the writing process. Besides *The Art of Teaching Writing* by Lucy Calkins I would recommend *A Writer's Notebook* by Ralph Fletcher, *Writing Workshop* by Ralph Fletcher and JoAnn Portalupi, *A Fresh Look at Writing* by Donald Graves, and *The Writing Workshop* by Katie Ray.

At the end of that first unit we had cause to celebrate. We had finished our very first "publication" as a class. I hung all of the students' pieces on a bulletin board in the hallway for a few days before our celebration to give people a chance to read each other's work. There were sticky notes available so that students could jot comments and compliments and stick them to the work.

On the day of the celebration, we gathered up as a class in the hallway and formed a semicircle on the floor. We did not read our pieces aloud or invite anybody to join us. I knew in the future we would have opportunities to do those things; I wanted that day to be about our community only.

I passed out clear plastic cups filled with Sprite so we could toast, as many writers do when they finish important pieces. After explaining a little bit about how a toast works, we all raised our glasses towards the writing pieces in front of us. "Here's to our first publication of the year and all of our hard work. May this be the beginning of many more wonderful pieces of writing to come," I said. We clinked our plastic glasses before heading back to work.

Figure 1–7a A Historical Fiction Piece from Unit on "Living the Writerly Life"

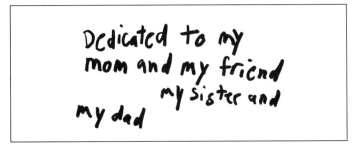

Figure 1–7a Continued

"I see land mama." Elizabeth said, scurrying to the deck where her mom was. "We're almost there, we're almost there!" she said leaping with excitement. Then the captain said, "We are heading for Ellis Island. Get your balongings." When Elizabeth got of the boat she saw lots of people from different contries. This is gonna be fun she thought. Then they got to a docter who checked in her ears and eyes. She followed the people down the path. She turned around and her father was signaling to come back. So she did. Her dad told her, "That docter checks everybody who is new here for diseases. He found one in your mother's ear." Then Elizabeth said, "Well, if she can't stay, I'm not staying." Even though she regretted it. But her father pulled her along the path. She turned to say bye to her mother, but she was already heading back to the boat.

"Today is my first day of school." Elizabeth said to her father when she was getting dressed. When she got to school her teacher said, "Class, we have a new student. This is Elizabeth. She's an immigrant from? Where did you say you were from?" "Poland" Elizabeth said proudly. Everyone giggled. Every day she tried hard to make friends, but everyone said she talked funny or they smirked when she passed. Finally, she couldn't put up with it any longer. She had to do something, but what? "I know I'll make something up!" Elizabeth was great at making things up. So the next day of school, when someone laughed she said, "I wouldn't do that if I were you." "Why not?" they all said. "Because, "Elizabeth replied, "I know the King and Queen of Poland and I could have you arrested." She didn't like to lie but she did see the King and Queen once. So from then on nobody bothered her. Actually, she became popular in school and people became fond of her.

Weeks went by and things were normal again until one day Mrs. Brian said, "class we have a new student. This is Antonia. She is from Brazil." Antonia spoke with an accent. Elizabeth laughed with all the other children. She thought it was quite fun to tease this new girl. But one day Elizabeth was lounging in her bedroom looking at the picture of her mother. She remembered her first day of school and how difficult it was for her. Then a thought hit her about the new girl, Antonia. She realized that what had happened to her was happening to Antonia. She remembered how sad she felt. Then she thought about how popular she was and she decided to make everyone stop being so cruel to Antonia. So the next day when ever somebody laughed she'd make them stop and apologize. So pretty much all was well. Elizabeth and Antonia became best friends. They told each other how hard it was to move and they were happy they had something in common.

Figure 1–7a Continued

Then one day something so incredible happened. Elizabeth and Antonia were walking home from school and Elizabeth was telling Antonia about how her mother was sick and had to go back to Poland. They were so lost in thought that they bumped in to a women. Elizabeth looked up to say sorry and when she saw who it was she gasped. It was her mother. She was almost speechless but she managed to ask her mother how she got back and how she got better. Her mother said that she never went back to Poland. She just stayed in the hospital and got better. It wasn't a big deal. She had been looking for them for days. Elizabeth showed her mother the way home and they rejoiced all the way there.

Figure 1–7a Continued

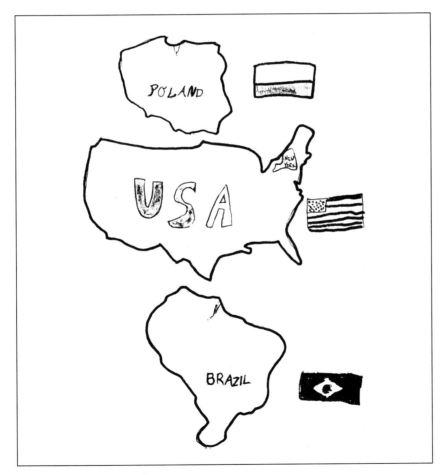

Figure 1–7a Continued

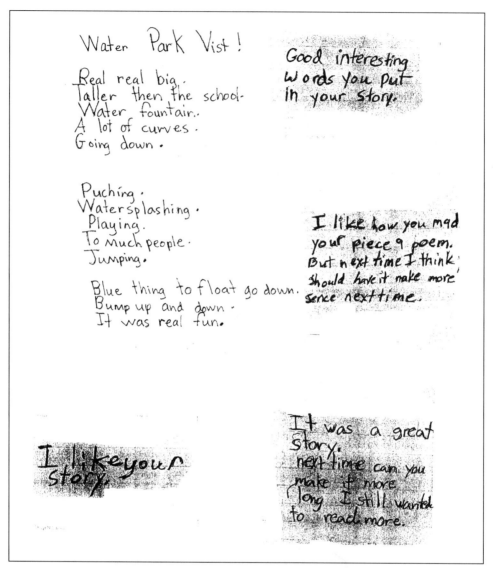

Water Park Vist !

Real real big.
Taller then the school-
Water fountain.
A lot of curves.
Going down .

Puching .
Water splashing .
Playing .
To much people .
Jumping .

Blue thing to float go down.
Bump up and down .
It was real fun.

Good interesting
words you put
in your story.

I like how you mad
your piece a poem.
But next time I think
should have it make more
sense next time.

I like your
story.

It was a great
story.
next time can you
make if more
long I still wanted
to read more.

Figure 1–7b A Poem from the Unit on "Living the Writerly Life"

Step Four: Studying Writing Conventions

I chose to follow up the somewhat amorphous study in living like a writer with a more concrete and somewhat traditional approach because, first, I believe it gives the students' caregiver's a feeling of confidence that students are mastering some basic skills. Second, I like to know that I formally taught certain conventions early in the year so that I can hold the students accountable for those conventions.

Figure 1–7c Students Toasting Their First Publication

Many teachers like to build a base of solid writing skills early in the school year. These skills can then be relied upon as a foundation for the more advanced skills that will come later in the year. One of my fourth-grade colleagues, Bonni Suslowitz, begins the year with a study in paragraphs and the thought process writers go through while determining when to make new paragraphs and how to structure them. Another colleague focuses on sentence structure, studying the importance of punctuation, transitions and meaning. I like to focus on punctuation, partly because I can work it into my teaching of other conventions, such as sentence structure, and also because I think punctuation has a huge impact on the quality of writing a student produces. In any event, when students are taught basic conventions they will not be as likely to be held back from writing by their inability to use them.

My punctuation study was short, about seven to ten days. In that time I taught mini-lessons on a variety of topics, always allowing the students time to try new punctuation moves while also practicing their notebook-keeping skills. The mini-lessons I taught during my punctuation study included:

- Reasons writers use punctuation
- Red lights and yellow lights: periods and commas
- Exclamation points and questions marks—a little goes a long way
- Dashes
- Parentheses

- Ellipses
- Colons
- Quotations marks

And if I'm feeling really brave . . .

- The Semicolon

Students then wrote a quick piece using punctuation in interesting ways. I offered the option to revise the first published piece with punctuation in mind.

Step Five: Making Sure the Foundations Are Sturdy

I believe that a child's developing into an independent writer is a very natural occurrence, and that it happens to many people outside of the confines of a classroom environment. But it can be difficult to teach an entire class full of children with different life experiences, strengths, and learning styles how to become even more independent without having some common ground. Before beginning to teach about leading independent writing lives I found it helpful to make sure most of the students have a few basic prerequisites in order to keep teacher "chicken with her head cut off" syndrome to a minimum.

My students needed to have a solid sense of how the class's writing workshop went:

- They needed to be comfortable with the writing process and have gone through all the steps at least a few times with teacher and peer support.
- Students needed to have a decent amount of material in their writers' notebooks with which to find independent ideas.
- It was also helpful if students had partnerships set up so that supportive peer relationships could be built upon.
- Students had to have access to and have read a rich variety of texts from a variety of genres so they were better able to envision their writing possibilities.

By the end of October we had completed our first three units and most of my students had the sorts of experiences just mentioned. We were ready to begin our first unit on independence. I planned to start with a kind of pep rally rather than an explicit lesson in writing independence. I knew that the more excited they were in the first few days of the unit the more willing they would be to work through the hard stuff. Then I would teach them the basics of how a writer independently navigated the writing process, something many students had no previous experience with. Finally, I would teach them about the logistics of independent writing such as proposal writing, setting deadlines, and pacing projects. I found that this introductory unit took between two to three weeks, depending on my students' previous experiences.

Diving into a Unit on Independence

The following chart is one possible way the independence unit can go (Note: the modifications column refers to any students who could use additional support, and should not be limited to students who have been identified as having special needs.):

Day	Topic	Mini-lesson	Modifications	Possible Trouble
1	Intro to Independence	Introduce possibilities and tools	List of possible genres and forms students can write in	Some students find this too amorphous—need conference
2	Intro to Independence	Introduce proposal sheets and give definition of deadline	Proposal sheet might need to modified	Students being unable to flesh out entire project idea by self—need partner
3	Topic Choice	Writers need to write *about* something, not just focus on genre.	Might need a checklist for students who need guidelines in writing	Some students might be so lost in the genre that they have forgotten the substance—need conference
4	Genre and form Choice	The genre can be shown in a variety of forms that best match the topic	Same list as day one would be useful	Some students may have hard time differentiating between genre and form
5	Writing Process	It's important to go through a process to write something so that it is fully realized	A mini-chart with steps of process to tape in writer's notebook	Some students tempted to skip spending time prewriting in a writer's notebook or doing necessary revisions
6	Writing Process	Knowing when it's time to move to the next step	A few might need a checklist to monitor this	Some students are unwilling to move on unless everything is "perfect"
7	Writing Process: Nurturing an idea	Writers spend a lot of time thinking about and playing with an idea before moving to draft	Examples of different ways to nurture an idea (besides writing in notebook)	Some students only know a few strategies to use—whole class share
8	Deadlines	Writers need to make realistic deadlines	Model using a calendar wisely	Students often over or underestimate deadlines—lots of modeling

Day	Topic	Mini-lesson	Modifications	Possible Trouble
9	Deadlines	Writers pace themselves	Discuss students work pace and help them use a planned amount of time each day as a means of pacing	Some students under or overestimate time needed
10	Writer's Notebook	The role it plays in independent work	Photocopies of examples	Some students have left notebooks too early
11	Mentors	Mentors are invaluable when writing independently	Paired-down list of mentors that match with certain genres	Some students need help finding mentor on own—have supply ready
12	Peer Conferences	Independent Writers need people to bounce ideas off	Model and/or list of expected partner responsibilities	A few students might have difficulty finding productive partnerships—teacher intervention
13	Peer Conferences	Ways fellow writers can help each other	Modeling and/or role playing	See above
14	Self-assessment	Writers reflect on successes and areas to improve	Modified self-assessment form	Some students have difficult time honestly assessing—conference

On the first day of our unit introducing independence, I walked them through all of the items available on the Silver Shelf that the students had yet to explore. The students had eyed the supplies on the lower shelves curiously since the first day of school but had only made use of the looseleaf paper and writing folders. I gave the requisite warning about misuse of supplies. They nodded solemnly.

Then I told them that from now on, when they had free time in the writing workshop, or at break, or at home, they could create anything they wanted in writing. In order to help them envision the possibilities I talked about things that my past students had published: cookbooks, plays, songs, and letters to a dad who was living in another country. I pretended not to notice the whispers that traveled through the room.

I gave them their only caveat. While they knew by then that it was possible to skip a step in the writing process, they needed to be able to explain how they were able to do that. I said, "The problem I see most writers come across when they first start writing independently is they skip the 'about' and jump right to the 'what'.

Figure 1–8 The classroom transforms into a flurry of activity when the independent workshop is in motion.

What I mean is someone will immediately say they want to make a picture book, but then realize that they didn't spend enough time in their writer's notebook thinking over what this picture book is going to be *about*. I know you guys won't get stuck in that trap, but I thought I'd warn you about it anyway."

Then I sent them off. The first day was filled with happy mayhem. I gave them little direct instruction, mainly a motivational speech to fire them up. My work was cut out for me in my conferences: field questions and plant ideas for future teaching.

Two boys, one prodding the other to go first asked the most popular question of the day, "Can I work with a partner?" It was a logical question. There's a comfort in exploring new territory with someone else, even more so when your teacher just announced she is throwing you into the wilderness of independent writing.

I answered, "You know that would be great. A lot of writers like to work with partners. It's nice to bounce your ideas off of somebody else and split the work up. Just remember it can be a little hard too. You're going to have to compromise a lot. Also, you need to make sure that you both have work you can do when you're not together."

I watched the partners high-five after my conference. I realized that they might be getting the impression that they could spend the year only doing half the work on their independent pieces. "Oh yeah," I added, "Don't forget that some of your independent pieces need to be written by yourself. Okay?"

I expect problems whenever I begin a new unit of study. Independent writing was no different. Many of the students would be doing what Australian educator Brian Cambourne calls "approximation," trying out something new that they had seen modeled by an adult. Just as we do not immediately correct a child who says "ba-ba" instead of bottle, we also need to accept approximations with literacy. I knew I would need to treat these conferences with a bit of fake nonchalance so that students felt their first stumbles were absolutely safe to make. Since I knew that troubleshooting would take up a large part of my conferences for the first few days I needed to keep these ideas in mind.

I said to Nili, an ambitious student who planned to write a novel, "Wow, that sounds great. I'm glad you have such great plans. It takes a long time to write a novel. Some writers even take years. I don't think the school year is a long enough time to give yourself for your novel. Since we want everyone to publish independently a few times in the year, maybe you can come up with other projects that you can do. That way you can work on your novel, but you still can publish this year too. I'll be happy to meet with you when you have a few sample chapters." The practice of accurately judging the feasibility of one's project is something that will come up again and again over the course of the year.

As I conferred with students, I reaffirmed the parameters I expected them to keep in mind. Those parameters were set based not only on my goals, but on my loftiest hopes and the things I knew I would and would not be able to tolerate. I think it's important to have a clear vision of your parameters before beginning to teach a unit in independence. That way when you are conferring and the unexpected comes up you will be better prepared to make those snap teaching decisions.

During the next few weeks I taught a string of mini-lessons all geared toward helping the students publish their first independent pieces. I also found it helpful to revisit these lessons throughout the school year.

- *Deadlines.* I modeled a letter to my mom for her birthday, using a calendar to plan out how many days it would probably take me to finish my independent project. I talked through paying attention to other deadlines, noticing days I had plans, and leaving a day or two for unexpected events. "Today is Monday, and I still need to draft and revise, so I think I can say I'll be done by Friday," I said.

   On another day I discussed pacing and how different steps in the writing process took different amounts of time. For example, I probably needed more than one day to work on revisions, but my first draft would only need one day. Even more complicated, different types of pieces took different amounts of time. Writing one letter to a pen pal was going to take less time than writing an article about the study results of the effects of light and soil on a variety of bean plants.

- *Nurturing.* Nurturing an idea takes time. Writers need to think about their topic, the genre they think makes sense, what ideas they need to include, and in other ways make sure that they are completely ready to draft. I needed to visit this step in the writing process several times in a year. It never seemed to be as sorely needed as when my students first embarked on their independent work. They could hardly wait to *make stuff*. The fact that they needed the content to be worthy of their product idea was difficult for them to grasp. And if this was not emphasized again and again, I might have found myself with plotless comic books, cookbooks with missing ingredients, and newspapers without facts.

  I taught a mini-lesson on different strategies writers used to nurture, or develop a new idea, such as: writing short entries in a writer's notebook, talking to a writing partner, researching facts, drawing pictures, and just thinking about the idea. I told them that many writers nurture an idea for years before they even begin drafting, so it made sense that the least we could do was spend a few days on it.

- *Writing Process.* Many of my students considered themselves writers, but most of them had relied on the teacher's curriculum to dictate their genres, deadlines, and in some cases, topics. Usually the stage of the process they were in was dictated by where the rest of the class was. They needed mini-lessons and conferences to teach them how to move themselves through the writing process.

  I found it very helpful to use a student from the class as an example. If Aidan had written fifty pages in his writer's notebook and completed two pieces describing the time his father got locked out of the house in his underwear, Aidan was probably able to spend less time in his notebook before drafting a poem about the same incident. However, if Aidan wanted to write a song about his dog he needed to go back and spend some time observing his dog and taking notes.

- *Peer conferences.* For my class this was the time when students realized the value of their peers. They had talked to writing partners for as long as they could remember, but that had always included the safety net of knowing the teacher could swoop in and save them if their partnership wasn't working out so well.

  I told them that most were going to finish several independent pieces over the year that I wouldn't see until they were officially handed to me. The only place left for them to get the kind of support that every writer needed was from other writers. They needed to be taught peer conferring skills in order to effectively edit each other's work, offer suggestions, and listen to each other. We went over a few easy-to-use strategies during this lesson such as listening skills, positive ways to give feedback, and body language. (I'll get more into this in the chapter on building a writer's colony.)

- *Choosing and Using Mentors.* Published writers as mentors were the keys for my students to learn how to be independent writers. In some years I have taught a unit on choosing a mentor author before formally introducing independent writing so that students had those skills mastered before beginning to work on independent projects. Other years I have found the stronger choice was to teach the unit after we studied independence, as a reinforcement of the role of mentors. I will go into more detail about that unit in the next chapter.

  There is always room to revisit and impress upon the students the impor-tance of mentors when working independently. Some students have a difficult time making the connection that models are crucial whenever working on a project, but especially when there is no whole-class study going on. I make sure to teach that as a mini-lesson during the first unit on independence.

- *Genre and Form Choice.* Writing comes in a variety of genres such as science fic-tion, mystery, and editorial. When we walk into a book store or library we are able to find the things we want to read based not just on the topic, but also the genre. When teaching that everything a writer creates for her independent work needs to fall into a genre, I like to make the distinction that writing also comes in a form. Sometimes the form and genre overlap, as with poetry. A poem is written in poetic form. Other times the genre can come in a variety of forms. A mystery can be in the form of a short story, a play, a letter, or even a picture book. I find that when students are explicitly taught the distinction they are more likely to write pieces with a strong sense of form and genre, as opposed to an amorphous piece with neither. [See handout on Form and Genre.]

- *Writer's Notebook.* The writer's notebook is a vital ingredient in all this work. I looked to published writers, my own writing and my students, to figure out how to best teach how a writer's notebook should be used while working on independent projects. I allowed my students to guide me toward what I needed to teach next about the writer's notebook by observing their work and listening to their talk.

  During the first unit of study on independence, I made sure to touch on writers' notebooks at least twice. First I talked about it as a valuable tool to use while nurturing an idea for a project. The second lesson involved offering a plethora of other ways the notebook helps to serve independent writers, such as keeping ideas for new projects organized, offering a place to jot down plans and practice new writing techniques, and keep research notes. (See Chapter 3 on the Writer's Notebook for more teaching ideas.)

The First Independent Unit Ends

In a way it was like taking off the training wheels. I set a date a few weeks after the formal unit was over for all students to have at least one piece of writing finished. This was possible because I had set the deadline for their first independently finished publication, though if they needed an extension or knew they would finish before the deadline they just needed to let me know. Although one could argue it was not strictly independent work because I had taught daily mini-lessons to support the work as well as set the first deadline, it was still work about individually chosen topics, in chosen genres, with chosen mentors. I also knew that for their first venture into independence territory a bit of handholding would allow them more autonomy later.

I looked over the pieces before the celebration and marveled at their variety.

- The two boys who had asked me if they could work together had created a how-to book on learning simple Japanese phrases.
- Ruthie had finished the first book in her "Magic Marker" series, a picture book about an otter who finds a talking marker. She had already begun work on the next book in the series.
- Kenya took a break from her play and wrote a letter to her grandfather who had died, telling him about what she had been up to.
- Aidan had written a poem, an ode to our class catfish, which he posted next to their tank.
- Nili decided to put her novel on hold, and instead ended up writing a historical fiction short story about a girl during the Holocaust.
- Oscar published his first comic book in his "Super Guy" series, to rave reviews. Despite the fact that it did not contain much text, he had certainly developed an exciting story line and a dastardly villain to hold his classmates' interest.

After looking through the pieces, I posted them on our bulletin board dedicated from that day forward to the display of independently published pieces (see Figures 1–9a, b, and c). Just as we had a celebration after we completed any unit of study, we needed to take time out of our hectic days to celebrate this first foray into the world of independent writing. Every unit of study seems to lend itself to a particular kind of celebration. In our first, we toasted our accomplishments. For this celebration I thought it was important that we writers gathered together for a little self-congratulation and very honest talk about how it went.

We began by gathering around in a circle on the rug, like the group of exhausted yet satisfied writers we were. We talked more at this celebration than any other we had all year. Compliments flew around the room, like "Lisa, I never knew tulips were so complicated." And, "Jake—your comic book is so funny!"

We talked about what was the hardest (trying to do everything in a short amount of time) and the best part (working with other people). Then after we had finished up our self-congratulations we talked about what was next.

"Well guys, you can tell from the class calendar that we're studying feature articles next. The thing is, even though in class we're going to be studying feature

Figure 1–9a An Independently Written Song

articles, I'm still expecting you to write independently. Talk to somebody next to you about how you can keep doing this fabulous work." I listened in as they brainstormed.

Eric turned to Aidan, "I think I'm going to try that list thing. I'm gonna make a list at the back of my notebook so I don't forget all my ideas for different pieces."

"I need a partner to work with. Want to be my partner?" Kenya asked her friend.

At the end of our celebration I handed them their gift: a calendar I photocopied for each of them to keep in their writing folders. It was fairly simple. I designed the card stock cover with a few hand-drawn decorations and their names written in silver ink. I explained that the calendar would be a powerful tool for them to carry through the plans they had just discussed. They could set deadlines, keep track of their lists of projects, set appointments for meetings with partners and balance it all with our class deadlines. Yes, that was right—I expected them to continue to publish their independent projects for the rest of the year.

Figure 1–9b A Science Fiction Picture Book, *Zerk and Bomby vs. The Earth*

③

"So anyway when are we going to try to take over earth" asked Bamby "today" Zerk said.

④

So they both got in the ship and went to take over earth.

⑤

"So how long will it take to get to earth" asked Bomby "I don't know" Zerk said "Maybe a hour or a half hour"

⑥

Bamby-"Why do we have to try to take over earth?" Zerk-"Because it says so in the alien handbook"

Figure 1–9b Continued

Figure 1–9b Continued

Figure 1–9b Continued

Figure 1–9c The First Book in the *Magic Marker Series*

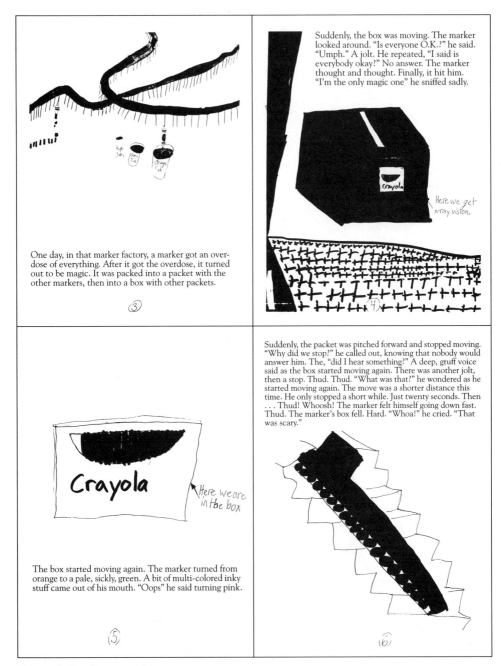

One day, in that marker factory, a marker got an overdose of everything. After it got the overdose, it turned out to be magic. It was packed into a packet with the other markers, then into a box with other packets.

③

Suddenly, the box was moving. The marker looked around. "Is everyone O.K.?" he said. "Umph." A jolt. He repeated, "I said is everybody okay?" No answer. The marker thought and thought. Finally, it hit him. "I'm the only magic one" he sniffed sadly.

Here we get x-ray vision.

④

The box started moving again. The marker turned from orange to a pale, sickly, green. A bit of multi-colored inky stuff came out of his mouth. "Oops" he said turning pink.

Here we are in the box

⑤

Suddenly, the packet was pitched forward and stopped moving. "Why did we stop?" he called out, knowing that nobody would answer him. The, "did I hear something?" A deep, gruff voice said as the box started moving again. There was another jolt, then a stop. Thud. Thud. "What was that?" he wondered as he started moving again. The move was a shorter distance this time. He only stopped a short while. Just twenty seconds. Then . . . Thud! Whoosh! The marker felt himself going down fast. Thud. The marker's box fell. Hard. "Whoa!" he cried. "That was scary."

⑥

Figure 1–9c Continued

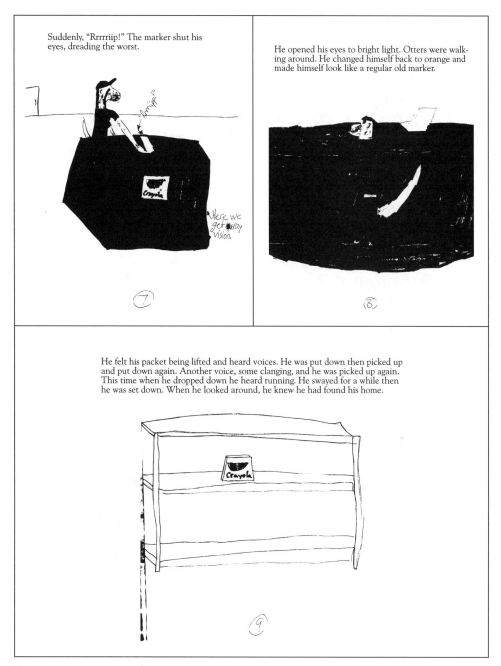

Suddenly, "Rrrrriip!" The marker shut his eyes, dreading the worst.

He opened his eyes to bright light. Otters were walking around. He changed himself back to orange and made himself look like a regular old marker.

He felt his packet being lifted and heard voices. He was put down then picked up and put down again. Another voice, some clanging, and he was picked up again. This time when he dropped down he heard running. He swayed for a while then he was set down. When he looked around, he knew he had found his home.

Figure 1–9c Continued

Resources for the Student Writer

- A few copies of thesauruses with varying levels of difficulty.
- A copy of an adult dictionary. *Webster's* paperback works well.
- *Writer's Express: A Handbook for Young Writers, Thinkers and Learners*, written and compiled by Dave Kemper, Ruth Nathan, and Patrick Sebranek.
- *Write Source 2000: A Guide to Writing, Thinking and Learning*, written and compiled by Patrick Sebranek, Verne Meyer, and Dave Kemper.
- *The Kid's Guide to Good Grammar*, by Dorothy McKerns and Leslie Motchkavitz.
- *So, You Wanna Be a Comic Book Artist?* by Philip Amara.
- *Becoming A Writer*, an edition from *Appleseeds*, co-editors Susan Buckley and Barbara Burt.
- *How a Book Is Made*, by Aliki.
- *When I Grow Up, I Want to Be a Writer*, by Cynthia MacGregor.
- *Writing Smart Junior: The Art and Craft of Writing*, by C. L. Brantley.
- *A Writer's Notebook: Unlocking the Writer Within You*, by Ralph Fletcher.
- *How Writers Work: Finding a Process That Works for You*, by Ralph Fletcher.
- *Live Writing: Breathing Life into Your Words*, by Ralph Fletcher.

Exercise Books

Not to be confused with writing prompts and not for all students, these books can help students practice their skills, get over writer's block, and get a jumpstart when working with a new genre.

- *A Writer's Notebook: How to Write Scary Stories*, by Kimberly Weinberger.
- *A Writer's Notebook: How to Write Poetry*, by Kimberly Weinberger.
- *A Writer's Notebook: The Ultimate Guide to Creative Writing*, by Pamela Curtis Swallow.
- The series of books called *Road to Writing* are particularly helpful for struggling students.

2
Finding and Using Mentors in the Independent Workshop

Nili, Letty and Cara huddled in the hallway with the *Park Slope Courier*, our local paper, spread out in front of them in messy highlighted and annotated pieces. In their laps they held clipboards filled with pages of paragraphs, cross-outs and post-its. They spoke in hushed voices, referred to their marked up calendars, flipped through notes and actively ignored me. Nili, the most vocal in the group, used her "To Do" list to check off each finished task. Their class newspaper was well on its way and they didn't need me.

Over at Table 2, in front of the aquarium, Ruthie sat by herself with only two things in front of her, the drafts of her short story and a photocopy of a poem. She stopped writing every once in awhile to stare at the catfish in the tank or glance back at her mentor poem.

In the center of the room on our large aqua rug, Aidan, surrounded by his materials, talked with Eric. There were index cards, looseleaf sheets of paper, and a few assorted cookbooks. Aidan pointed to a brightly colored cookbook. "You see, what I'm going for is something like this. Can you do this for me? I have those little introductions before each recipe and I would really like it to be in color." Eric nodded and made notes on a handwritten draft of Aidan's work.

Oscar, usually overwhelmed by writing, walked up to me waving a pile of papers, a huge smile on his face. "I'm going to work on football. There's a new rookie on the Giants and I want to write about him." He disappeared, a *Sports Illustrated for Kids* tucked under his arm.

There's a Proverb That Says . . .

When I was in high school, the English teacher I idolized, Mr. Kopacki, shocked us one day when he said, "I live by the saying that a teacher knows he has done his job when his student no longer needs him. In fact, when the student becomes the master and the master becomes the student then the teacher can truly be satisfied." Even though I was fifteen years old, a time when I thought I knew everything, I was still pretty surprised that Mr. Kopacki would ever want to give up the mantle of master and allow his students to become the teacher.

Now that I am a teacher, I see how primary that goal is in my practice. The central point to our teaching of independence should be to teach our students how to write without us. The best way to accomplish this goal is by introducing them to the writing community. This community will be made up of friends, critics, and colleagues. It will also be made up of mentors.

The mentors I will talk about in this chapter are not the ones many of us think of when we hear the word "mentor"—the older, wiser, in-the-flesh people who personally guide us by example, advice, and nurturing. Although I hope that all of my students will eventually build just such a relationship with another writer, I know that those relationships are rare and hard to come by. Instead, the mentors discussed in this chapter refer to the role of professional writers, their work, and how that work can mentor our students to learn by example.

The ability to find and learn from another writer will serve our students far beyond the confines of our classroom. It allows Aidan to write cookbooks even if there are no friends to cheer him on. All he needs is Julia Child and some paper. It allows Oscar to create comic books, even if he's no longer allowed to write them in middle school. *Calvin and Hobbes* will suffice. It allows Ruthie to write letters to her father, even if she does end up moving to another country, far away from her language, her school, and her teacher.

Writers travel well.

Learning from a Mentor Author

Writers read a lot. They read for enjoyment, to learn new things, and to learn about writing. Writers don't just need to read books about writing in order to learn how to become better writers. Writers can also learn about writing by reading in order to study the craft of the text.

It is that work of "reading like a writer" that literacy educator Katie Ray talks about in her invaluable book *Wondrous Words*. She explains how students are able to use their reading to become better writers. I highly recommend reading her work if you have not already had a chance. She explains in depth and with eloquence the importance and the practical implications of learning about writing by reading. In this chapter I will briefly describe the way I taught my students to read like a writer in order to be mentored by published authors.

When most of us pick up a book we have certain goals: entertainment, research, diversion, and so on. At other times we read as writers. How was this made? What did the writer of this piece do to make this sentence so strong? Why did this title catch my eye? When we read with questions like these in mind, and then study the text with an eye to improving our own writing, we are using that author as a mentor. For example, I admire the way Jane Yolen can write anything from a historical novel like *The Devil's Arithmetic* to a memoir picture book like *All Those Secrets of the World* with a sense of lyricism. I might study a piece of her writing that really stands out for me. I'll read it a few times and notice the way she uses sentence length and verbs to help make her sentences more rhythmic. Then, when I go off into my own writing, I would try to lengthen some of my sentences and use more verbs and fewer adjectives to try to connote the sense of lyricism I admired in Jane Yolen's work.

When I first taught my students how to use a mentor author, I modeled daily, and had my students try the strategies I modeled with the same author I was using so that we had as much cohesiveness as possible. I made sure to read the text first for enjoyment, so that we could all read the text as readers first—as the author intended us to do. Then, because many of my students had done this kind of work before, I modified the inquiry chart that Katie Ray refers to in *Wondrous Words* and made a large whole-class version (Figure 2–1). As a class we spent a few days and studied the text in depth, using the chart to guide our inquiry. When we were done, we were able to immediately apply what we noticed our mentor did to our own writing.

Of course, we did all of this work very much all together. Most of my students were able to study a mentor author and use the author to help raise the level of their writing, as long as I told them which author to study and reminded them frequently to use the mentor author. But we needed to become more independent than that. After all, when the students went off to work on their own projects I wouldn't be around to help them.

Choosing Mentors Independently

All of the mini-lessons mentioned in the first chapter are hugely invaluable in the beginning of a study on independence. But the single most valuable topic for both the teacher's sanity and the students' autonomy is learning how to find, choose, and learn from a mentor.

Two different ways I have used over the years to teach my students about choosing mentors come directly from the work of Isoke Nia (literacy staff developer and nationally renowned speaker) and Katie Ray. While there are several other possible teaching choices, I found that depending on the year, one of these two worked best with my students.

I found the first approach useful when working with a class that needed more explicit instruction and modeling. There is a strong structure in place that allows

STUDYING A MENTOR AUTHOR

MentorAuthor: _____		Title of Mentor Text: _____	
What are some of our favorite parts of the piece our author wrote? (The Good Writing)	Why do we think the author decided to write like that? What does it do to make the piece better?	What do we want to name this writing move?	Have we seen another author write this way? Where? Give an example.

Figure 2–1 Favorite books and their authors can help guide a student's decision to choose a particular mentor text.

for students to be exposed to a large number of good mentor candidates in a short time. It is also helpful for people who feel a little overwhelmed by the number of children's authors students may choose from as mentors. Teachers are able to choose the authors they know best and might feel less anxious about having to contend with a large variety.

I found a second approach useful when working with a class that, on the whole, had a lot of experience with using mentors and did not require as much explicit exposure to a variety of authors. It is also fairly easy to weave this string of lessons into a unit introducing independent writing. In the end, it may be a mix of the two approaches, or something else entirely that works best for a specific class.

The most important thing is that our students are taught in a fashion that enables them to master the skill of learning from other writers so that they are able to best write independently.

One Option for Teaching Independent Writers About Mentors

Working with Isoke Nia in her Leadership Group on Independence in the Writing Workshop at Teachers College Reading and Writing Project, I learned of a more structured way to introduce my students to choosing and using a writing mentor than the way I had used in the past. Isoke suggested that learning how to choose a mentor author should be taught as a mini-unit of study. I discovered that if I placed the unit towards the beginning of the school year, my students developed valuable skills they immediately put to use while working on their independent writing projects.

To begin, the students had to know how to actually look closely at a text and use it as a mentor. (No one explains this process better than Katie Ray in *Wondrous Words*.) I started out by modeling the process using a whole class shared reading piece—Cynthia Rylant's *Scarecrow*. We read the familiar piece again, this time as writers looking for the parts that we really loved in her work. Then we charted our observations as well as our theories about Cynthia Rylant as a writer. These days were more whole-class activities than mini-lessons, since we worked all together using one author. After spending a lot of time studying the different crafting techniques Cynthia Rylant used in *Scarecrow*, we moved into the most exciting step—trying out her techniques.

"I like the way she used 'ands' a lot in the sentence: *The earth has rained and snowed and blossomed and wilted and yellowed and greened and vined itself all around him*," Jeffrey said. He then took a deep breath before sharing how he tried out Cynthia Rylant's crafting moves. Jeffrey's sentence in his writer's notebook read, "My brother ran and fell and rolled and played and tripped, but it did not end there."

After I made sure everyone understood the idea of applying a mentor author's techniques to their writing we moved on to phase two. A few days before, a fellow fourth-grade teacher, Kate Pollock, and I spent an afternoon getting prepared. First we made a list of authors we thought would make good mentors. We wanted to have at least six to eight authors to choose from. Together we developed criteria for what we were looking for. We wanted an ethnically and culturally diverse group of writers. We wanted each author to have written in at least three different genres. We also wanted them to have written at a variety of different reading levels and to be authors our kids would enjoy reading. In the end our list included Gary Soto, Jacqueline Woodson, Jane Yolen, Eloise Greenfield, Kevin Henkes, Laurence Yep, and Karen Hesse.

Then the fun began. We scoured our classroom libraries, our colleagues' libraries, the schoolbook room, and finally the school library. In the end, not surprisingly, it was the school library that gave us the most resources. We found books we hadn't even known our authors had written, such as short stories in anthologies. We also collected biographies and autobiographical articles for each author. In the end we had a basket for each author that included between three to five pieces (at least one of these was a chapter book) and a photocopy of biographical information. We thought the chapter book was particularly important because a majority of our fourth-graders were reading chapter books—they needed to know how to navigate using them as mentors.

Our next two mini-lesson/writing periods were dedicated to the kids getting a chance to roam around the classroom, sifting through the various author baskets and reading. I began with a brief mini-lesson that explained what our goal was—to learn how to choose a mentor who they thought was a good fit for the piece they were working on. I talked about why there were different genres in each basket and why there was biographical information. I also talked about why Kate and I chose the authors we chose and let them know that if there was a particular author they loved, who had written in a variety of genres, who was not in a basket, to let me know and I would make up a basket for that author. The last part is an important option to offer students, since our objective, even before we introduce the concept of "independence" is to give our writers lots of independent choice. In my class Laurence really loved Roald Dahl and felt that his adventure story would benefit from Dahl's influence. We had a brief conference and I decided to make up a basket for Laurence's author after Laurence had taken some time to explore the other authors. No one else wanted Roald Dahl, and no one else decided to choose another author, but it made their decisions much more independent to know that they *could* choose outside the baskets if they wanted to and knew why they wanted that author.

We also set up the ground rules: no more than five people at one basket, make sure to try out at least three authors before making a final decision, and you need to be able to explain why you chose that particular author. Since the baskets were spread out on tables and the meeting rug, students gathered in temporary clusters to work. Most kids carried their writers' notebooks with them, taking notes about certain authors' lives, their writing, and what might make them (or not make them) a good mentor (Figure 2–2). Students who wanted or needed modifications used a sheet with general guiding questions on it (Figure 2–3). There was a lot of talk between the students as they worked, "Hey Aaron—I think you might like Laurence Yep. He has a mystery over here and you're writing a mystery"; or "I can't believe how totally different each one of Jane Yolen's books is. I bet she wrote every genre there is" (Figure 2–4).

Our share sessions on those days were filled with lots of thoughtful "writery" ways of talking. Nili announced, writer's notebook open in her lap, "I've been tak-

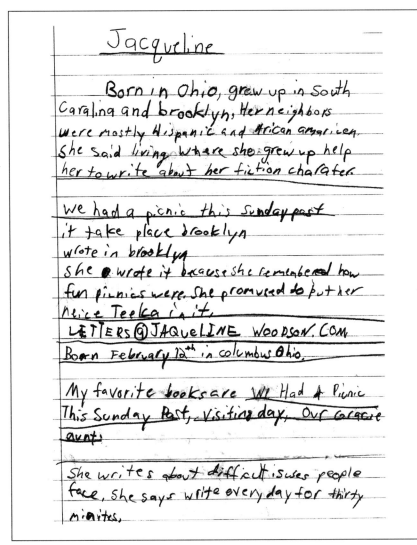

Figure 2–2 Notes from a Notebook Taken as the Student Explored Possible Mentors

ing notes about the different writers, and even though I've only read in Laurence Yep's basket and Karen Hesse's basket, I already think I'm going to pick Karen Hesse. She just has such smooth writing and I love the way her characters sound."

Eric was bursting at the seams, "I thought for sure I was going to pick Jacqueline Woodson because I love all her books so much, but then I read Eloise Greenfield's stuff, and I really like the way she uses rhythm and capital letters in her poems. They make you read loudly or softly and they have a beat. I think I want my poems to do that."

Learning about our Mentor Author

1. The author's name: Eloise Greenfield

2. When was the author born? May, 17, 1929 in Parmele

3. Where was the author born? North Carolina

4. What can you find about what your author was like when she/he was a child? She and the other children in the housing Project played games, Also she played in the fire hydrant showers They played Joperope to entertain them shelve.

5. List five other interesting facts you learned about your author:

   1. She wrote nonfiction and fiction and picture books,

   2. she has a son and dauter

   3. She wrote 38 books including Picture books

   4. She as won lots of rewards from her writing,

   5. She grew up in Washiton D.C

6. What do you notice about the author's writing? What kinds of things (genres) does the author write?
The author writes fiction, nonfiction, Picture books

7. What topics/subjects does your author write about?
Her subjects are black kids book

8. Where do you think (make a theory) your author gets his/her writing ideas?
I think she gets ideas from seeing kids do activity.

9. Now take some time to look through all the stuff your author wrote and choose one text that you would like to use as a mentor (example) for your own writing. It should be a piece that you would like to write like. What piece did you choose? By myself Why did you choose this piece: Because I picked By my self is because I sometimes I be by myself.

Figure 2–3 Handout with Questions to Help Focus Student Mentor Exploration for Students Who Need Modifications

Figure 2–4 A student spends time studying Jacqueline Woodson.

After those few exploratory days (my class took about two sessions and Kate's took about three) we made our final selections and began to think about how to apply what we knew from the whole class's study of *Scarecrow* to our work with mentor pieces. With the help of parent volunteers we gathered the texts of picture books, short stories, and selected chapters from the bigger books so that every student could have a copy of his or her own first choice.

Our next few mini-lessons walked the students through the process of studying their mentors up close and then using what they learned in their drafts and revisions. This work was based on the modeling I had done using Cynthia Rylant's *Scarecrow*. Students filled out personal versions of the whole-class chart using their chosen mentor (Figure 2–5). During their independent work time we had many conferences and small group meetings dealing with such difficulties as leaning too heavily on the mentor (using the exact same wording or topic as their mentor) and how to use a chapter book (by choosing one chapter to really study).

After the students had gone through this process with a lot of teacher and peer support, they had a pretty solid idea of what to look for in a mentor, how to study a mentor, and how to use their mentor's crafting techniques. Granted—the students would still need some reminders and help throughout the year—on the whole they had a very good idea about how the whole mentor thing works and could complete this task fairly independently.

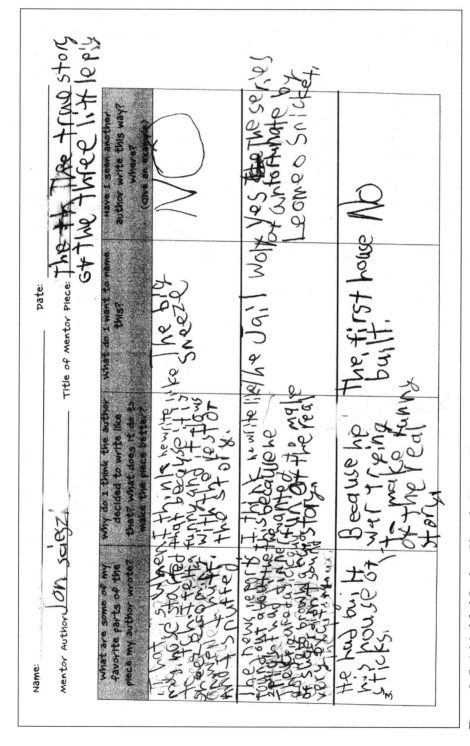

Figure 2–5 A Modified Student Chart for Mentor Text

ONE POSSIBLE WAY THE MINI-LESSONS COULD GO

Day	Topic	Mini-lesson	Modifications?	Possible Trouble
1 & 2	Reading like a writer	Revisit reading like a writer by studying teacher's mentor text and charting what was noticed	Personal copy of text for students who have difficulty focusing on overhead as well as small copy of whole-class chart	Some students have difficult time understanding how to read like a writer. A lot of modeling is necessary
3	Using a mentor text	Revisit using a mentor text to craft own writing	Some students might need help picking the parts of their own writing they would like to try using a mentor with	See modification
4–6	Exploring mentors	It is important to explore a variety of mentors before choosing one. Students will spend the next two to three days looking at several options before choosing one mentor	A sheet with focus questions to help students who have a difficult time with the open-ended aspect of taking notes in the writer's notebook	Some students are reluctant to look at other authors as soon as they find one they love. Other students have a hard time pacing themselves
7 & 8	Reading like a writer	Making the connection between whole-class experience and the student's chosen mentor. Students chart their work	The chart might be modified for ease of use	Going through the process more independently can be difficult
9–?	Using a mentor text	Making the connection between class crafting work and individual work with chosen mentor	Peer and/or teacher modeling	Going through the process more independently can be difficult

Another Option for Teaching Independent Writers About Mentors (and giving them a peek into their teacher's head)

My students have studied the craft of writing at the knees of Donald Crews, Cynthia Rylant, and Sandra Cisneros since kindergarten. They know how to pull apart a piece, study it, name it, and then try it on for size. The scary thing for most of my students is not using a mentor. They know how to look closely at another writer's craft and figure out how to use those crafting moves in their own work. It was the sifting through the endless possibilities to find the perfect mentor match. It was looking through a few possible writers and choosing the one who does the best job with what the student is struggling with. It's deciding what the *really* good writing is and how a person manages to figure out where to fit that *really* good writing in her piece.

I started off this somewhat daunting teaching task by reminding the panicked ones that they knew a lot. They'd been working with mentors since forever. Kenya countered with, "Yeah, but our teachers always gave us our mentors. They made copies and put them on overheads and stuff. How are we supposed to do that?"

Kenya had a good point. I knew that I had already done a few different exercises involving mentors, and each time I dutifully pulled out the piece, copied it for everyone, made a copy for my overhead, and together we charted everything we noticed. Of course I made a point of explaining why I chose each one and how I found that particular author. I had also given them choices of different mentors for different pieces, each time with suggestions like, "Your piece reminds me a lot of Jacqueline Woodson's *We Had a Picnic This Sunday Past* because of your strong sense of voice and how you use so many different characters. I was thinking you might want to look at the way she connected those things in her piece and see if something like that would work for yours."

Don't get me wrong. I think those are good teaching moves. These moves even made it possible for Kenya to ask her question. We had a common language and a common understanding from which to work. Now my responsibility was to show her what I had been doing, to give her the insider's view to the teacher/writer's mind.

Throughout our teaching we make a point to share our thoughts as learners, writers, and teachers. We take the mystery out of what we're doing and by doing that we empower the students. I've always made a point to connect students over and over again with Good Readers, and Good Scientists and of course Good Writers. It is important to validate their work by making them aware they are part of a community larger than the confines of our classroom. I also make sure when teaching a lesson on any topic to talk about myself as a learner. "I know when I learned this division method I was so excited because long division had been so hard for me. Now it seems so easy I can't believe I was ever stressed about it."

In fact, I am guilty of not always telling them the true, exact reasons why I made the teaching choices I made in writing—why exactly I decided to start our year by studying how writers live during our unit on "Writerly Life" and why I made sure we were doing our nonfiction genre study before the ELA (the very important fourth-grade New York State English Language Arts test) was not always up for discussion. Now, I'm not saying I need to bore them with every little detail of my teaching decisions, but there are things that would serve them well and there is really no reason for me not to share them.

One of the best ways to start this process of demystifying teaching is during the study of independence. As teachers, when we study independence, we offer our young writers the tools to create their own writing lives outside the teacher's watchful eyes. It is a natural progression to explain our thinking. The easiest way for me to begin is to talk about mentor choice.

"Kenya asked an excellent question yesterday. How *are* you supposed to find mentors when your teachers have been doing it for you all along?" I said this not knowing what the response was going to be from the class. They nodded and sat up straight. Clearly it was a question many of them shared with Kenya.

I continued, "Today I'm going to try to answer that question using my own experience of looking for a mentor. I know that when I needed a mentor for my feature article on the legalization of ferrets in New York City, I went through several steps. Let me tell you what I did."

I showed them a chart that read:

How Do I Choose a Mentor?
- READ A LOT!
- Look for authors I know and love and eliminate everybody else.
- Think about how I want to write and try to find a match.
- Narrow down my choices to the same genre.
- Listen to other writers' suggestions.
- Wait to make a final choice until I know the writer really well.

I was a little surprised and very impressed when most of my students copied down the chart in their notebooks. It was something I had noticed more and more—the things they were learning were becoming more valuable to them because they were invested in their work and they knew they were expected to do the work independently. Those future solo efforts made them more interested in keeping track of the lessons.

I followed that mini-lesson with a very similar lesson the next day. This time the chart read, "What Do Writers Look for in a Mentor?" I began the lesson saying, "Okay, so yesterday we started answering Kenya's question. I still think that we could use a little more help. After all, yesterday we talked more about how to look and where to look. Today let's talk about what it is we're looking for when we're looking for a mentor."

The kids used their experience from yesterday's workshop, and together we created a new chart. They had tried some of the things from yesterday's lesson and knew they had valid contributions to make. The chart we created together ended up reading:

What Do Writers Look for in a Mentor?

- The Mentor's style reminds you of yourself.
- But the mentor's work can't have the same seed idea or topic.
- You like their structure.
- The length of the piece is close to yours.
- The language is like yours.
- The genre is similar.
- You *really* admire them and love their writing.

The last point was very important to my class. Just as with a good friend, it's important to really like someone if we're going to spend a lot of time together. We were going to be reading the mentor pieces over and over. It was important that we loved that piece so much that we wouldn't get sick of it. Ruthie loved Jane Yolen. She constantly brought me books by her favorite author. There was no book she loved more than *The Ballad of the Pirate Queens*. She carried it around with her constantly. She loved the story and admired Jane Yolen's skill so much that this piece became a natural mentor fit.

Of course, despite all of my talk about this independence thing being all in their hands, that I was going to theoretically go on a writing teaching vacation, I was working overtime. I knew from experience that this first dip into independent waters would require a lot of support from me.

They needed help mostly with the choice of mentors as opposed to how to use a mentor as a model. This help varied from simply directing them to a particular shelf in our class library ("Go take a look at our magazine basket. You might find something there") to bringing a small stack of possible mentors to a conference and walking the student through the selection process. For the most struggling writers, I often offered a choice between two familiar texts. That way, although they might not yet be capable of digging through all of our resources to find the perfect match, they still had some power of choice (Figure 2–6).

Kenya and her friend Soroya were two students who needed more direct teaching in order to choose a good mentor. They were not quite proficient readers and tended to stick to series books and one or two favorite authors. While this would be great for their reading life, this made the pool of possibilities they could draw on from memory much smaller than writers with a more varied diet.

When I noticed the pair having a heated discussion I pulled up a chair next to them. It turned out that they were arguing about what mentor they should use for their piece. In front of them were tried-and-true mentors like *Chicken Sunday* and *When I Was Little*. "What's going on guys?" I asked.

Figure 2–6 Some students find it helpful to work with other students as they look for a mentor author.

Soroya blurted out, "We can't find a mentor for our play. We looked every-where. So since our play is about a family I picked out these books but Kenya says they're not plays so we can't use them."

It made sense that they were having a hard time finding playwrights to use as mentors. Most of my class's play collection was buried in anthologies. I made a mental note to create a basket dedicated to plays. Then I said, "Kenya's right that those aren't plays. A play is the kind of thing that is really specific in the way you write it out. Hold on." I returned with two of my favorite plays. I knew that for these two girls, with their limited experience reading plays and their struggles with reading, handing them a huge assortment of plays would only have made things more complicated than they needed to be. If they decided they didn't like either play I offered I could find them others, but I had a hunch they would choose one of the ones I suggested.

ONE POSSIBLE WAY THE MINI-LESSONS COULD GO

Day	Topic	Mini-lesson	Modifications	Possible Trouble
1	Choosing a mentor author	It's important that independent writers choose their mentor authors	Vocabulary support for students who need it	Some students might feel a little over-whelmed when the announcement is made

Day	Topic	Mini-lesson	Modifications	Possible Trouble
2	Choosing a mentor author	Demystify process by discussing steps teacher went through	Personal copy of whole class chart	
3	Choosing a mentor author	What do writer's look for in a mentor? Chart the characteristics		
4	Choosing a mentor author	Ways to narrow down the search for the perfect mentor	Pre-narrowed-down mentors so students having a difficult time can choose from a few good matches, as opposed to the whole library	Some students will need teacher and/or peer support to navigate this process

A Note About Conferences

Conferences become an axis upon which independent writing revolves. Students need that personalized support in a way that they never have before because it is more than likely that the teaching going on in the mini-lessons, while applicable, does not directly address the issues each individual writer is grappling with. Carl Anderson, in his practical book *How's It Going?*, does an excellent job of discussing the importance of conferences and how to skillfully implement them in the classroom. It is a valuable resource for conference work.

Conferences about mentor choice are vital because students are in effect choosing a teacher for themselves. It is important for us to make sure that the choice will allow the student to reach all of his or her writing goals. When I met with my students during this study I liked to carry around copies of a few different texts I knew really well and were pretty versatile. That way it was easy for me to guide a student right to a specific mentor if that was the trouble they were having. I also kept a mental checklist of things to keep in mind while talking to a student:

- *Genre.* What genre was the student planning to write in? Sometimes a student is unsure of the genre so he or she has a difficult time deciding on a genre. Other times a student doesn't realize that a mentor text needs to be in the same genre. Sometimes the genre a student wants to write in does not have an immediately accessible mentor available in the classroom, and the student needs help either choosing a more common genre or locating a piece. (One good source for mentors from a variety of genres is *Free to Be You and Me*.)
- *Length.* Students in the upper elementary grades primarily read chapter books. Unfortunately, most fourth-graders do not write with the length or complexity of the pieces they read the most. This can be frustrating for some students.

Figure 2–7 Regularly conferring with students allows the teacher to steer them toward mentor texts that will be good matches.

They might need to be led to short stories or other pieces they have little experience with. Another option is to find a book where a chapter can stand on its own, and use that single chapter as a mentor.

- *Quality.* Frankly, some of our students' reading diets are less than ideal. While I wouldn't argue against a little "beach reading" when relaxing, there are certain texts that are not good models. The words used are redundant, the story structure might be simplistic, or perhaps the characters are shallowly depicted in some of the texts that students are considering. These books certainly serve a purpose in a child's reading diet, particularly if they are of high interest. But in the beginning of learning how to use a mentor text it will be difficult for students to spot good writing they want to emulate if there is not much good writing to be found within the text. Sometimes we need to steer our students toward texts of better quality, which have characteristics similar to other less desirable texts (action, humor, genre, etc.).

In addition to the conferences, I have also found it helpful to create a chart for students to post the mentor piece that they chose alongside the project they were working on. The chart has enabled me to do a quick check of students' status. It also has allowed other students to see other mentor possibilities.

Troubleshooting

Once students began to write independently, they automatically turned to mentors whenever they began a new project. While the mentors they chose varied from student to student, the motivation was the same: to make the best piece possible a writer needed to study other writers. An unexpected benefit of the independent use of mentors was that studying a mentor's work became a part of many students' instinctive writing processes.

Not every student made that transition so easily. I needed to regularly check on the status of mentors in my students' writing lives. Important questions I asked myself regarding my students use of mentors included

- *Are my students using mentors in ways that improve the quality of writing?* Most of them were. There was no question that Oscar had a sense of story development and comic book voice which came directly from his mentor, *Captain Underpants* by Dav Pilkey. However, there were still times when students would have a weak point, like the ending of a piece, and not immediately think to check to see how their mentor ended the piece. That was something I could easily teach a mini-lesson about.
- *Can my students accurately choose a mentor that's right for each different piece?* I found a more mixed bag on this one. Some students still insisted on using mentors, which were writing pieces far beyond their means (such as J. K. Rowling). Other students consistently chose excellent mentors and in fact even introduced me to a few. It was a student who introduced me to Jack Gantos' book, *Joey Pigza Swallowed the Key*, which had a first chapter that many students used as a mentor when writing fiction. To help students who were still struggling with mentor choice I would confer with those students, sometimes putting together a group conference if there were enough students with similar needs.
- *Are my students' needs being met by familiar mentors or do my students need to be introduced to a fresh crop of writers?* Most of my students were able to find what they needed from our class collection of mentor texts. There were a few however (the very strong and the very struggling) who needed different mentors. I made a point to have conferences with those students as soon as I could, sometimes directing them to undiscovered mentors in the classroom library or to my own collection of mentors.
- *Are my students establishing bad habits such as only writing the same kind of pieces with the same mentor, or choosing mentors they're tempted to copy?* This was something I had to be vigilant about. There were a few students who still had a difficult time differentiating between research and mentorship. Letty wanted to write a picture book for her sister about wolves, but after she had taken all the facts she could from a few different resources, I noticed her drafts sounded sus-

piciously like Seymour Simon's *Wolves*. Letty was not intentionally copying Simon's work. She was simply having a difficult time making the distinction. We worked together to find another nonfiction picture book that had nothing to do with wolves to use as her mentor but still had the characteristics she was looking for.

What Happens to a Class That Uses Mentors?

Fast forward to March: my class hoarded good mentors like a pirate's booty. Any piece of text I copied they filed away in their writing folder for future use as a mentor. If I used a text and hadn't made copies for them, like an editorial about school uniforms from the newspaper, there was always at least one student asking, "Could I get a copy of that?" It was fabulous side effect that I had never expected. My students became pack rats of other writers. Not only were they collecting their own words and ideas in their notebooks, but other writers' as well. Their writing folders were truly becoming writers' filing cabinets. They contained the drafts and assessment sheets they always carried, but now they also carried the work of Eve Bunting, Thomas Locker, and Charlotte Zoltow.

Other marvelous things happened. Because they were constantly on the look out for a good mentor, they knew a lot about what was in our library and could help other writers in their search for mentors. "Colleen, where's *Just Juice* (one of our class read-alouds)? Nili is looking for a piece that has a country sound to it. I said she should look at that one," Cara said. After her conversation with Cara about the book, Nili decided that Karen Hesse's *Just Juice* was a perfect match for her. She liked the strong voice of the narrator, as well as the little turns of phrase like the ones in the following passage:

> Ma puts a sandwich into each of our three bags and folds the bags shut. I like how neat those folds are. It is like unwrapping a gift, opening the bag at lunchtime. Even after I've used the bag all week and it's as limber as a dishrag, I still like opening it and taking out that jelly sandwich every morning, even if I don't end up eating it in school the way she hopes. (Hesse, 1998, 2–3)

Nili spent lots of time loving, studying and living with Karen Hesse's words, and the influence of Hesse's "country sound" is evident in this excerpt from her piece, "Pa's Knockin'":

> Suddenly I started sneezing like a dog's barkin' in the moonlight, howling and crying like a baby's cry in the wind. I knew somethin' was wrong because, any time I start sneezing constantly, it means something's wrong. It sounded gray, gray as the lint balls in your washer and dryer.

Ruthie chose Thomas Locker's picture book *Water Dance* for its unique way of dealing with a nonfiction topic, the water cycle. She liked the rhythm in his writing, which is almost like a call response, and in first person:

> Carried by the winds
> from distant seas
> I move,
> growing heavier,
> growing darker,
> returning.
>
> *I am the storm front.*
> (Locker, 1997, 17)

Ruthie captured that lyrical tone, as well as the first-person voice when she wrote her piece, "Mars: The Red Planet":

> Long ago my blood was hot, it burned through my skin, poured out
> and mounded on top of my red, hot, steaming body.
> That mountain was Olympus Mons.

Another pair of students was clearly influenced by Dav Pilkey's combination of prose, comics, and humor (see Figure 2–8).

Once again, writers as mentors proved to be invaluable sources in the workshop. Trying to balance my planned curriculum with myriad independent projects in the works would have been a Herculean task if not for the help of my faithful writer friends. Students were able to learn structure, language, voice, style, and the characteristics of a genre with nary a word from their teacher.

Intro

In the country of country there is a town called: The town where sunny and Russ live with bad guys and the bad guys do bad things vill. Where our two heroes were born and raised by their creator named Bob Short And Fat. The man who sunny and Russ is fighting is trying to take over the world one frying pan at a tine.

Figure 2–8 A Partnership Created This Book, *Sunny & Russ*, While Using *Captain Underpants* as a Mentor

Figure 2–8 Continued

Figure 2–8 Continued

Figure 2–8 Continued

Figure 2–8 Continued

Figure 2–8 Continued

Figure 2–8 Continued

Figure 2–8 Continued

Ways to Find Mentors

Besides choosing mentor texts mentioned in this chapter here are a few other places to look:

- *Wondrous Words* by Katie Ray has numerous suggestions for mentor texts.
- Children's magazines such as *Sports Illustrated for Kids* and *National Geographic for Kids* have short nonfiction pieces.
- Children's periodicals such as *Cricket* and *Cobblestone* offer a mix of genres to choose from.
- Some short story collections and children's anthologies center around a certain theme. (*Free to Be You and Me* is an excellent source.)
- Picture book text is often similar in length to the pieces our students write.
- The school librarian often knows of the latest collections and periodicals. Ask her to keep an eye out for you.

3

When the Writer's Notebook Becomes the Writer's Notebook

Every year, after the winter holidays, I always feel as if my students are fully, officially, fourth-graders. Unfortunately for me, it is also easy to mistake the comfort and maturity that comes around that time in the year as mastery of everything I have taught so far. I simply assumed that after learning about and successfully living as independent writers and successfully navigating the complicated world of mentors, they would have a handle on what I considered the more obvious things. After all, for a few months they had managed to balance our whole-class curriculum while simultaneously working on independent projects. It seemed to me that they were independent writers who were masters of their domains. But I found out that I needed to rethink those assumptions and, in the process, embark on my own learning journey.

"Okay Aidan, does that make sense to you? Let me know how it goes," I said with a sigh. Aidan trotted happily off. I was ready to bang my head against the table. It was January and his was the third conference in a row about choosing what to write about. It was dangerous for independent writers to be grappling so regularly with something that was so key to writing. It didn't make any sense to me why year after year, month after month, students struggled to find something to write about.

The casual observer might say, "Hey, writers get writer's block all the time. These aren't even adult writers. Give them a break." But as writing teachers, we know that the acceptance of writer's block would be the death knell for our writers' workshops. We wouldn't accept "math block" or "reading block"; the same must be true for writing in school. I would also argue that professional writers, that is, people who make their living from their writing, cannot accept writer's block either. For now, its best to establish that learning is our students' job, and writing is one of the many things they must accomplish in order to earn their "paycheck" (getting smarter).

Besides, if they are to lead independent writing lives, they need a ready source of ideas flowing, and the logical tool for harvesting those ideas is the writer's notebook.

In addition to all that, my students had kept writers' notebooks since they were in third grade, some since second grade. They knew the writing process inside and out. They had written everything from memoirs to poetry. They had notebooks filled with entries. Yet, here they were stuck. Something was wrong. It was a writing classroom emergency.

More Problems

My original instinct was to focus only on the issue of my students struggling to find rich topics to write about in their notebooks, which would lead to creating pieces with a clear focus. But once I got to talking and thinking about this one notebook problem, I started to unearth other notebook problems.

I asked my colleagues about their experiences. I wanted to know if I was alone in this quandary, or if the issue was more widespread than my classroom. Not surprisingly, in grades where students used notebooks, teachers noticed their students dealing with the same problem my students were dealing with. What's more, once I opened the conversation, there were other problems with writers' notebooks that teachers had noticed cropping up in their classrooms:

- Notebooks were filled with the same kinds of entries on the same topics without going deeper.
- Because the composition book (the size I recommended to my students) was so large students rarely carried it anywhere other than home and school— further reinforcing the idea that notebooks were for school work only.
- Notebooks read more like a run-down of each day's events with no reflection or emotional involvement.
- Notebooks were stuffed with sketches that went nowhere.
- Notebooks that were used like draft paper. There were only completed drafts of poems, stories, and articles.
- Notebooks were by the book—the only writing in them is assigned and purely what the teacher asked for, no more.

Not surprisingly, all of my colleagues' notebook concerns turned out to be the ones I had also grappled with in my classroom. Before I even began to solve the problem, I had to make sure I knew exactly what I expected from my students' notebooks so I would best know how to direct my teaching.

So, What Is a Writer's Notebook?

This is a controversial question in some circles, and an absolutely benign one in others. Notebooks come in many forms, names, and styles. There are journals, idea books, logs, index cards, scraps of paper and the proverbial cocktail napkin.

Ralph Fletcher writes, "a writer's notebook is nothing more than a blank book, but within those pages you've got a powerful tool for writing and living" (1996). Some published writers I spoke to rarely go anywhere without a notebook and write in it religiously. Other writers never use a notebook at all. Instead they prefer to let ideas stew around in their mind until they are ready to draft.

Of course, as teachers we need to set some parameters and guidelines for our students to work in, otherwise the chaos that could ensue would override our best intentions to give our students an authentic writing life. Some of those guidelines we draw for our students must be indelibly drawn in Sharpie marker. Other lines are drawn in pencil, ready to be erased and tinkered with at will. When it comes to notebooks, I've found that my students are the most successful when I have given them a very clear definition, yet with flexibility clearly established.

So what *is* my definition of a writer's notebook? After much thought and a lot of reading about and talking to writers, I've come up with a working definition: a writer's notebook is a notebook where writers keep stuff that may or may not be used to make completed pieces in the future. The key in this definition for me is that the notebook is ultimately a tool put into service for the ultimate goal—finished pieces that people besides the writer will read. In some descriptions of writing processes the notebook falls into the stage called "prewriting"; in other descriptions it is an important tool throughout all stages of writing. Every writer's notebook is different and each is very indicative of the writer it belongs to. (I don't tell my students about writers who don't keep notebooks.) Consequently, our teaching about notebooks needs to be as flexible as possible to meet the needs of all our writers.

Experienced Writers and Their Notebooks

After my conference with Aidan, and a lot of thought about the notebook problems students dealt with, I realized I needed to figure out a concrete way to address the issues students were having. Just as we looked to other writers as our craft role models, I needed to look at the way writers used notebooks. My first stop was the writer I knew best—me.

Probably the most grounding thing in my teaching career was to look not at my school writer's notebook that I used as a model for my students, but to look at the notebook I used for my own writing. It's something I suggest all teachers of writing who keep a notebook do at least once. The first thing I noticed is that I had not one notebook, but several, one for each project I was working on. I also had a small notebook I always carried in my bag to capture unexpected images and thoughts. Then I had a personal journal, as well as an ongoing idea notebook where I jotted down new project ideas as they came to me.

Next I noticed that, unlike my students' notebooks, all of my notebooks showed a huge variety in the length and types of writing that went in them. I had one-word notes to myself, lists, long entries that meandered, exercises, and—the largest difference—plans for future writing projects. To my horror, I realized that there were very few similarities between how I used my notebook and how I expected my students to use theirs. I did not write nightly in my notebooks. I only went to one of them when there was something for me to write in them. Except for my journal, all my notebooks were kept with an eye toward making something. I have a notebook for my adult novel, for my kids' novel, and for this book. I have another notebook where I'm just trying out ideas for future projects, everything from letters to my family to an article.

Of course, I know that I'm not the only example of writers and their notebooks, so I did a little more researching. There is a useful book called *Speaking of Journals* (Graham, 1999) that includes a variety of children's authors interviewed about their notebooks and journals. By reading the book I found out that Jacqueline Woodson (*We Had a Picnic This Sunday Past*) didn't keep an actual writer's notebook. Instead she used a journal to write about her life, people in her life, and events. She saw it as separate from her creative writing. Jack Gantos (*Joey Pigza Swallowed the Key*) started a new notebook every time he started to write a new book. "Sometimes what I do is write the fiction on one side of the journal, like a regular book, starting in, then I flip it over so it's upside down and I work that way on the personal life."

The more I dug, the more I realized that when I tried to hold my kids to a uniform structure I kept them from becoming the independent writers they could be. After all, the notebook is a powerful tool for writers, but I could only imagine how much further my students could go if they could design the tool to best serve their independent writing purposes.

After my epiphany that showed me the way to free my students from the tyranny of teacher-mandated notebook keeping, I also remembered they were children and they were in school. I needed to create a balance, just as I did in the other parts of independent writing. There would still be times when my students would use their notebooks in the way I taught for exercises and assignments. I would just need to balance that with their need to use their notebooks in their own ways as well.

Making Notebooks More Like *Writers'* Notebooks

Looking so closely at notebooks, a tool I had taken for granted for so many years, was both an exciting and humbling experience. Exciting because I unearthed so much new (for me) knowledge about notebooks and had really made the connection between what experienced writers do and what my students can learn from them. It was humbling because I could not believe I had taught so many students and never really studied the notebook and what it could help students achieve.

I also realized something I had suspected, but had not been entirely certain about until after going on my fact-finding mission: notebooks are different when writers are independent. They become more important. Once a writer establishes her personal goals she is using her writer's notebook with very specific purposes in mind, her notebook will often change. Some things I noticed about students' notebooks after they began working on independent writing, but before I had directly taught them about notebooks, included:

- The entries were more directed towards a purpose—a finished piece of writing that would go out into the world.
- The entries were not mindful of any audience, such as a teacher, but rather, reflected the writer's true thoughts, experiments, and scratchings.
- It was difficult to trace a logical line from entry to entry because they were written on an as-needed basis. The missing pieces were in the writer's brain, not in the writer's notebook.
- There were many more lists as the writer strived to keep her writing life organized.
- It was easy to trace the notebook entries that were connected to the whole-class studies and the ones connected to independent work.

I needed to cultivate and celebrate those changes in their notebooks because those changes were a visible sign of their budding independence. But I also knew that several of my students were not using their writers' notebooks in different ways because as far as they were concerned notebooks were whatever the teacher told them to do with them. It had never occurred to them that a notebook could be used as a powerful tool while creating independent work.

I think it is helpful to dedicate a few days during the first half of the school year solely to the writer's notebook. Just as with all strings of mini-lessons, it is important that the teacher decides what her students most need and directs her teaching to those needs. After doing my own research on professional notebooks, as well as researching what my students were doing, I knew I had to keep in mind that many of my students

- Had a narrow view of uses for the writer's notebook
- Were not making the connection between independent work and notebook keeping
- Saw the notebook as a mandated part of the writing process, as opposed to a useful tool within it.

Below is a string of mini-lessons I taught based on what I knew of my students and what I hoped I would be able to open them up to.

Assess What They Know About Notebooks

While I don't often use mini-lessons as a means to gather information, in this particular instance I wanted to facilitate a conversation about notebooks, both to get information about how my students were using them and to make clear that we were setting up a new world for our notebooks.

I began by telling the kids that I had been looking closely at writers' notebooks because I knew we could make them even more helpful. "You already know a lot about notebooks since you've been writing in them since at least third grade. Why don't we start off by you telling me what you know about notebooks?"

As they talked, I charted what they had to say. They started out talking about things they knew would make me happy:

- Writers use their notebooks every day.
- They contain memories, dreams, questions, images, overheard conversations.
- They're personal, not private.
- They're a place where you don't have to be perfect.
- Every entry should be dated.
- You nurture your ideas in them.

"Okay, those are all things we know about notebooks. Is there anything we can add when we think about our notebooks when we're doing independent writing?" Apparently so. After exchanging a few glances they added:

- They have lists.
- They have plans.
- You can keep notes in them.
- They help you keep your project ideas straight.

I read over the list with them and complimented them on how smart they already were about notebooks. "Starting today we're going to look really closely at our notebooks so that we can get even smarter. As a writer I'm always on the lookout for ways to make me smarter about writing. When I find something I think I should know more about I study it. That's what we're going to do for the next few days." I asked my kids to pay extra close attention to their notebooks and the work they did in them when they went off to work.

Comparing Other Writers' Notebooks

For the next lesson I thought it was important to give them another notebook, besides their own, to study. I highly recommend, keeping your own writer's notebook if you don't already, so that you are able to have first-hand experience with the work the students are involved in and are able to use it as a model for the students. Very few things make as large an impression on children as seeing their teacher model her own struggles and successes. That said, I realize that not every teacher has the time or inclination to keep a writer's notebook. Here are a few ways to still offer solid models for students to follow:

- Save a good writer's notebook from a past student who has hit most of the teaching points that will be covered in the year.
- Borrow a notebook from a student in another class who would be willing to let you photocopy select pages to share with the class.
- Find an example from a published writer the students are familiar with. *Speaking of Journals* has several useful excerpts to share with students with authors as varied as Jean Craighead George to Bruce Coville.
- Create a dummy notebook. This was something I did for years while I kept my real notebooks secret from my students. Make sure to include all the components that you want your students to have in their ideal notebook.
- Make photocopies of notebook entries that are reproduced in this book to share with students.

I began my lesson using my own writing experiences with one of my notebooks in my lap. "Today I'm just going to give you a brief tour of one of my notebooks, just so you can get an idea of some different things to try with your notebooks," I said. I flipped through the pages and talked as I went, "This notebook is for my kids' novel about Cesi, the girl who runs away to Mexico. Here's the one sentence that started the whole book (Figure 3–1). Here's a list of Cesi's quirks. Here's just a paragraph where I describe her walking out her front door (3–2). Here's a list of scenes I needed to write and a few notes to myself (3–3). Here's a chart where I tried to plan out the plot for *Border Crossing*. Here's some notes on the research I did about how to get from California to Mexico."

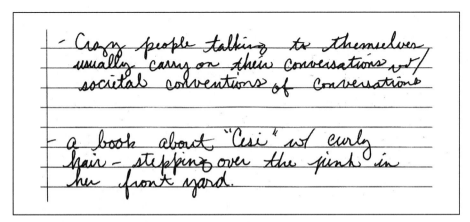

Figure 3–1 My Notebook Entries from *Border Crossing*

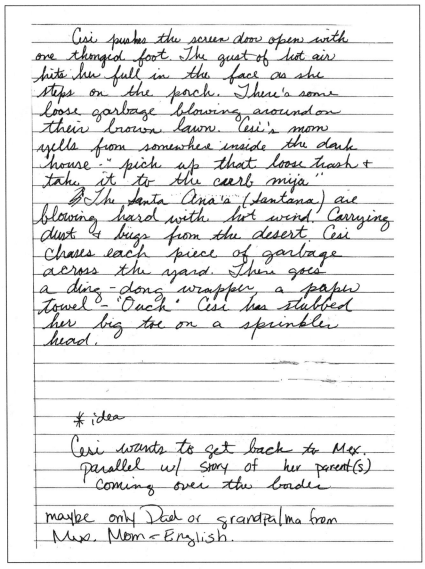

Figure 3–2 My Notebook Entries from *Border Crossing*

Nili was surprised. "I thought you'd have a lot more writing in there. I mean, you have one hundred pages in your draft so far."

"Yeah, it is surprising. But I'm a big list maker and jotter. Sometimes one sentence can become a whole chapter," I said. I talked through other sections of my notebook, making sure to explain why I chose to use my notebook in the particular ways I was describing.

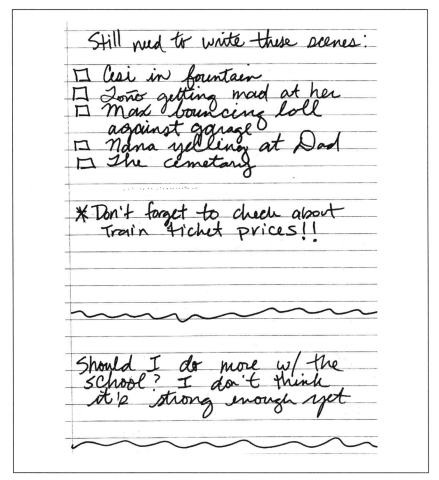

Figure 3–3 My Notebook Entries from *Border Crossing*

"Even though my notebook has a lot of lists and jottings, it's important to remember that every writer is different. One of my friends only makes charts. Another one of my friends writes pages and pages. Just like Jacqueline Woodson and Jack Gantos keep completely different notebooks, I don't expect anybody in this class to keep his or her notebook in exactly the same ways," I said.

Students' work that day was to pay close attention what made them feel most comfortable and productive when using their notebooks. When I had conferences with students I noticed that some students were already making changes. Some students were making t-charts, others were making webs. I saw a lot of list making, but I also saw short paragraphs and longer entries as well. By the end of the period, students came to the rug talking to each other about the type of notebook keeper they were.

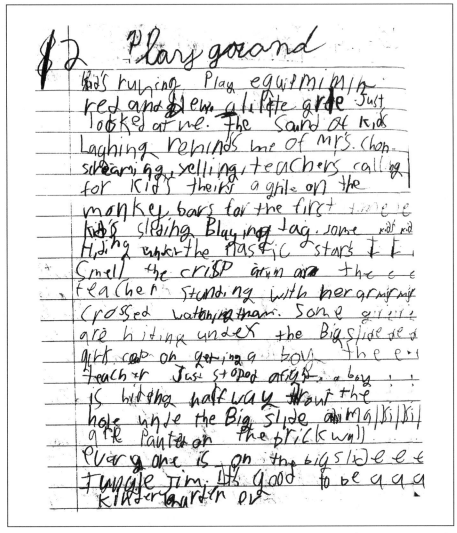

Figure 3–4a Before Looking at the Writer's Notebook, Most Students Entries Looked Similar

"Oh, I'm more of a jotter. I like to just jot a few words down so I don't forget my idea," Ruthie said.

Nili nodded, "I like to do that too, but I think I'm more into charts. They help me keep all my ideas organized."

"I still like to write long entries. I like saying everything I want to say all at once," Kenya said, reminding people that she was already on her second writer's notebook for the year.

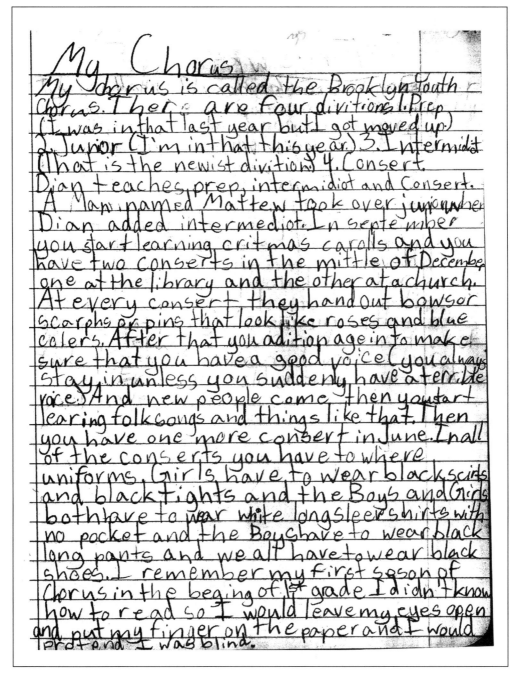

My Chorus

My chorus is called the Brooklyn Youth Chorus. There are four divitions 1. Prep (I was in that last year but I got moved up) 2. Junior (I'm in that this year.) 3. Intermidiot (that is the newist divition) 4. Consert. Dian teaches prep, intermidiot and Consert. A man named Mattew took over junior when Dian added intermediot. In september you start learning critmas carolls and you have two conserts in the mittle of December, one at the library and the other at a church. At every consert they hand out bows or scarphs or pins that look like roses and blue colers. After that you adition age into make sure that you have a good voice (you always stay in unless you suddenly have a terrible voice.) And new people come, then you start learing folksongs and things like that. Then you have one more consert in June. In all of the conserts you have to where uniforms. Girls have to wear black scirts and black tights and the Boys and Girls both have to wear white long sleev shirts with no pocket and the Boys have to wear black long pants and we all have to wear black shoes. I remember my first seson of Chorus in the beging of 1st grade I didn't know how to read so I would leave my eyes open and put my finger on the paper and I would protend I was blind.

Figure 3–4b Before Looking Closely at the Writer's Notebook, Most Student Entries Looked Similar

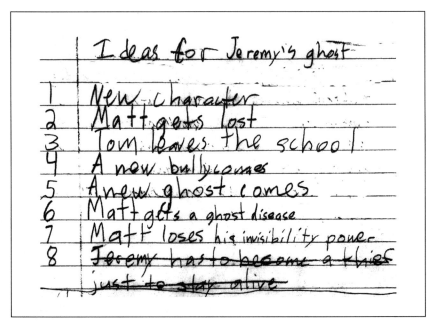

Figure 3–5a After Looking at the Writer's Notebook, More Variety and Individuality Was Apparent

Of course, many of the students were talking as if there was much more in their writer's notebook than there was. True, some students had been using their notebooks in self-designed ways, but most of them hadn't. Their talk then was more about their intentions and their ownership over their own writing style, their approximation, than it was about what was truly going on in their notebooks that day.

Uncovering Secret Notebooks

My goal for the next lesson was to continue with the work of revealing possible permutations of the notebook. I had no idea I was going to start a revolution. I began by saying that I had spent a lot of time studying notebooks lately and had looked at mine in particular. I showed them my stack of notebooks, the largest a composition book, the smallest the size of a wallet. I explained that the small one was convenient to carry around. The composition book I used mainly when I was going to write long about something.

Kenya, one of the most avid notebook keepers, shyly raised her hand. "I have a secret writer's notebook. It's really small and I always keep it in my bag. It goes

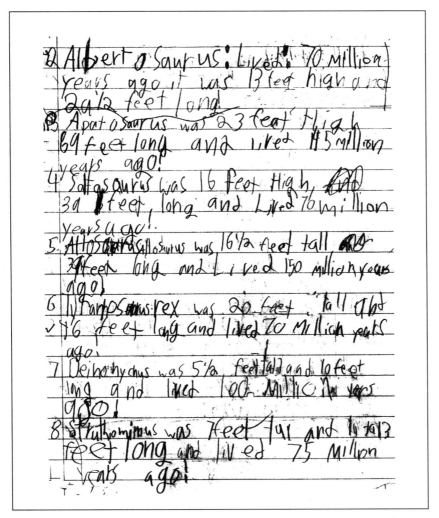

Figure 3–5b After Looking at the Writer's Notebook, More Variety and Individuality Was Apparent

everywhere with me so that if I get a really good idea I can write it down right then. I didn't know that was okay," she said.

"Of course it's okay. It's way more than okay. Kenya, you're doing exactly what professional writers do when you keep a notebook with you all the time. You can keep track of every little thing you want to write about," I said.

Kenya must have broken the ice, because several hands all flew up at once. "I have a secret notebook." "Me too!" I wanted both to pat myself on the back for

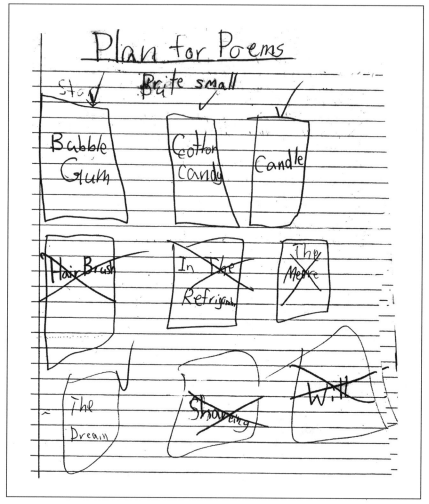

Figure 3–5c After Looking at the Writer's Notebook, More Variety and Individuality Was Apparent

making this discovery and kick myself for taking so long to give my students the freedom to discuss their underground notebooks.

I also discovered that most of the students had second, third, and even fourth notebooks that they wrote in regularly. They just never thought they were school-sanctioned. Just as when my students were exhilarated and surprised when I first introduced the idea of independence as a means to create new projects and bring into school the project they worked on at home, now they couldn't keep their places on the rug. They all had notebook stories to tell. Suddenly the official writing notebook was no longer confined to what the teacher expected. The secret notebook was free.

Of course not every year or every class will have secret notebooks. There might just be a few or none at all. That's okay. I have found that some years students will take the ideas I talked about and begin either creating "secret" notebooks, or do something to radically change the structure of their existing notebooks. What is important is that students understand that the writer's notebook is a tool they can use for their own goals as well as for the ones their teacher has set.

Using Our Notebooks as Tools

The next day, when we gathered on the rug for workshop, I noticed that many students had brought in "secret notebooks." There were sparkly gold ones, and tiny spiral ones that attached to key chains. I pulled my own out. "Well guys, I really feel like we are cookin' now. Look at all these notebooks." The students beamed like proud parents.

"Yesterday we discovered that some of us had been keeping secret notebooks and didn't even know they were okay. Today we're going to talk about what goes into a notebook. How we organize it, what we use it for and what we put in it, is just as secret for some of us as the secret notebooks were," I said.

I began by talking about the unique way Jack Gantos divided up his notebook so that his real life got sort of mixed in with his fictional characters. I talked about how Jean Craighead George (author of *Julie*) does a lot of sketching in her notebook. "You know that my notebook is a lot of jotting and a lot of lists. In other words, the way a writer keeps his or her notebook is unique to the way that writer works best. I write best when I've done a lot of thinking and jotting. I save my drafting until I can get to a computer. Writers use their notebooks in ways that will help them the best. If we are spending so much time in our notebooks that we have hardly any finished pieces, there's something wrong. If we are hardly ever using our notebooks and have a lot of pieces but they don't really seem to show much thinking, there's something wrong. We need to make sure that our notebook is used as a tool, like a hammer, that helps us write the best and the most we can write," I said.

Then I shared a chart with a list of different ways I knew writers used their notebooks as tools:

- Storing ideas for future projects
- Keeping track of characters
- Note-taking for research
- Recording results of a survey

- Sketching settings, objects or people
- Planning drafts
- Experimenting with sections of a piece, like a dramatic scene
- Recording interviews
- Listing things to include in a piece: scenes, characters, favorite words, etc.

After introducing the list I pointed out that there was plenty of room for the students to add other ways they used their notebooks as tools. Their work for the day was to try one of the things on the list they had not yet tried but thought might be useful for their independent work.

Writing Independently Makes a Writer Use His or Her Notebook Differently

I began the next day's lesson by confessing I had realized that my notebooks with the longest entries, the ones that would make the most sense to a person who tried to read it, were for projects I had never finished. My notebooks that had lots of strange little notes to myself, lists, sketches and charts, however, were for projects I was doing well with or had already finished. I realized that it was important to pay attention to how I used my notebook, but it was also important to consider why I was writing in my notebook.

"Which made me think that when I purposely go to my notebook so that I can work on a project that I *know* I'm going to finish, it's very different than when I go to my notebook because I'm bored, or I know I should because I haven't written in it in awhile," I said. A few students exchanged looks. Apparently I wasn't the only one.

"When we go to our notebooks because we want to, not because our teacher told us to, or because our grown-up said we had to do some homework, it is different. It even looks different." I put two pages from two different notebooks on the overhead. The first was a notebook entry I had made for school. The second entry was one I had made while working on *Border Crossing*, my kids' novel. I discussed the importance of purpose when going to a notebook. There was nothing wrong with going to a notebook because your teacher said you had to. It was just different. Students flipped through the pages in their own notebooks and talked about what they noticed about different sections. There was a different feel to entries that had to do with our last whole-class study on feature articles than there was to entries that were connected to independent projects.

I ended the lesson by reminding them that we needed to be sure we were clear on our purposes when we used our notebooks so that we got as much out of the experience as possible. Before the students went off to work, I had them turn and tell a partner what their intentions were for working in their notebooks that day. Just by making that small change in thinking about purpose, students were more productive that day.

A Writer's Notebook Is Not Everything . . . But It Can Help You Get Where You Want to Go

Because we were in the middle of testing season, it was easy enough for me to let the focus on the writer's notebook go for a few days. Instead I gave students an opportunity for a few periods of strictly independent writing time. There was no formal lesson, but I was around to talk with students. I did this partly because students needed a break from the formalities of test prep, and partly because I wanted to see if any of this notebook talk would help move independent projects along as I had hoped. Many students did move faster but more importantly, I observed several students regularly traveling with notebooks at the ready, drafting with a notebook beside them, and in other ways becoming more independent in their use of them.

By looking at writers' notebooks more closely in January we were able to breathe new life into something many of the students had taken for granted. We also discovered, as a pleasant side effect, that the better we were at making our notebooks work for us, the better we were able to reach our independent writing goals. On top of it all, many students made an important discovery when the secret notebooks were uncovered: if keeping a writer's notebook going at home was part of being an independent writer, then many of them had been independent writers all along without knowing it.

In our final lesson on the independent writer and his or her notebook I wanted to really ensure that students understood the possibilities of a writer's notebook. I began by complimenting them on their work over the past few days. I talked about different things I had noticed. Aaron was creating an outline for what looked like a novel and we had not even discussed outlines as a possibility. Oscar was drawing character sketches of the superheroes and villains he wanted to include in his next installment of his comic book series, "Super Guy."

I then introduced a new chart titled, "What Independent Writers Know About Notebooks." I had written the first item on the list, but held my marker ready to hear what they had to add. While I know that most mini-lessons need to be directly teaching students something, I thought in this particular lesson it would be helpful for students to learn from each other, as well as from me. When the chart was finished it looked like this:

What Independent Writers Know About Notebooks

- Notebooks are tools for their ultimate goal—the finished piece. *Notebooks = hammer and nails. Finished pieces = the table*
- Writers make their own rules for their notebooks—what works best for them.
- Long entries are there because the writer felt like she or he needed to write long.
- Jottings are good.

- Notebooks have lists of ideas for future pieces.
- Notebooks have "to do" lists for current pieces.
- Notebooks are great places for exercises.
- We put anything in our notebooks that we think can be made into something.

Students left this discussion feeling very confident that they not only knew a lot about the writer's notebook in general, but that they had a very good sense of how their own notebooks should go to best support their independent projects. The following chart illustrates one possible way a mini-unit on the writer's notebook can go:

Day	Topic	Mini-lesson	Modifications	Possible Trouble
1	Assessment	This is actually an assessment, more than a mini-lesson. What do students know about the writer's notebook?		Keeping all students actively engaged in the discussion so there is a good sense of what they know
2	Writer's Notebook	Introduce another writer's notebook	Students who need to see something up close should be seated near teacher	Some students might be defensive, and protective of their current notebooks
3	Writer's Notebook	There may be more than one way to keep a notebook . . . or notebooks: uncovering secret notebooks	See above	Some students might feel pressured to get an additional notebook. Make sure it is clear that writers create a notebook-keeping method that works for each writer
4	Writer's Notebook	Ways to "Use" our notebooks as tools	Students might need a personal copy of whole-class chart	
5	Writer's Notebook	Writing independently makes a writer use his/her notebook differently	Some students might need to see copies of different notebooks to see options	
6	Writer's Notebook	A Writer's Notebook is not the end-all be-all . . . but it can help you get where you want to go	Some students might need a personal copy of the whole-class chart	A few students might feel overwhelmed by the openness and need narrowed-down options

What to Expect from Notebooks from Now On

I knew that after looking at notebooks as a critical element in living an independent writing life, my students would no longer have "cookie cutter" entries, but ones that are personal and useful. I also saw that students either continued to have separate notebooks for independent and whole-class projects, or they somehow separated the two different worlds. Some students had whole-class projects relegated to the front of the notebook and all independent projects confined within the back half. Other students would jot a quick "I" with a circle around it whenever working on an entry that was meant only for an independent project.

The notebooks changed. They became a more active part of the writing workshop. They became more personal in use, not just content. They became as varied and unique in writing styles as the students were varied in their learning styles. However, the notebooks weren't completely controlled by the students. I still noticed a uniformity of sorts while we worked on whole-class studies. There were certain entries I could expect to find depending on the lessons taught. My expectations were still observable within the pages of the writer's notebook. But now my expectations were blended with the students' own expectations for their work.

A Few Books About the Writer's Notebook
- *A Writer's Notebook: Unlocking the Writer Within You,* by Ralph Fletcher
- *Breathing In, Breathing Out: Keeping a Writer's Notebook,* by Ralph Fletcher
- *Speaking of Journals: Children's Book Writers Talk About Their Diaries, Notebooks and Sketchbooks,* edited by Paula Graham

4

The Writing Colony: Building Community for Independent Writers

One Is the Loneliest Number: We Aren't Completely Independent

When I was an angst-ridden teenager with black fingernails and white lipstick, I romanticized the idea of Writer. I envisioned myself ala J. D. Salinger, alone in a one-room cabin in a remote forest. "Writers don't need anyone," was my mantra. My fantasy writer-self would write complicated and intellectually stimulating tomes, only stopping to double-check the spelling. I would need no revisions because I was an Inspired Artist, and everything that comes from an Inspired Artist's pen is flawless. My fantasy writer-self sent my novels off to the Publisher, who would send me large cash advances, and beg me to come meet my admiring masses. But I was a Writer. I lived alone. I worked alone. The only company I needed was the company of the characters I created.

Then I went to college and my writing professor, Perry Glasser, had lots to say about my writing. Everything that poured out of my pen was a lot less than flawless—it needed all the help it could get. It was my first lesson on how absolutely dependent writers are on other people—and not just their adoring readers.

In our regular day-to-day lives we need people to tell us if the red sauce needs more salt, if the picture is hanging crooked and if there's lettuce stuck in our teeth. In soccer, when a first-string player is tired, the coach subs in another player. "We need fresh legs," she'll say. In writing, we may be the player that ultimately scores the goal, but without fresh eyes, we won't be able to make it at all.

There are a lot of other reasons why independent writers need community. Here are a few I have thought of based on my own experiences in a writing community:

- *Deadlines/Accountability.* Knowing that I am going to meet with my adult writing workshop every week makes me stay on task. I don't let my teaching and social lives completely take over my writing life. When I was writing without the workshop, it could be weeks or months between writing times. When we give our students an environment where they are not only accountable to the teacher, but to their peers as well, they become more responsible writers.

- *Levels of Experience.* In my writing workshop there are professional writers who have published novels, articles, and short stories. There are folks who are trying their hand at their first novel. We see that sort of range in our students. Nili might have written three realistic fiction pieces over the summer while Oscar still struggled to include a setting in his short story. Yet they can work with, learn from, and inspire each other.

- *Shared Knowledge.* The world is full of experts. The interesting thing to me is that as writers, we aren't usually experts on the stuff we want to write about. When students have opportunities to be experts for each other, we not only help them to learn from each other, but we also offer opportunities to share the things they know a lot about and never realized could be useful to somebody else.

- *Problem Solving:* I have a problem with titles. I don't usually have a title for a piece until it's almost done. And even then, it's a painful process. How can I possibly come up with a few words to encapsulate something that took me

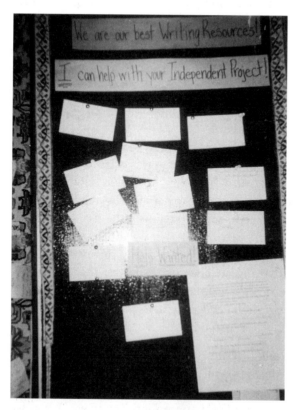

Figure 4–1 Our Interactive "Help Wanted" Bulletin Board

I know alot about
cats
Libby

fast If you want
I am Typing,
your person.
Contact alex F.

Marissa is available for
Illistrating. "Verry good at
Drawing" My mom says. I will
allso publish.

Figure 4–2 Posted on the "Help Offered" Board

Dear class 4-305,

_____ and _____ are looking for
actors and scene artists and stuff like that to help put on a play of
The Lion, The Witch and The Wardrobe. The play will be in front
of the whole school, and another performance will be done at night
in front of the parents.
  If you want to participate, please put the tear-off sheet below in
_____ or _____ mailbox.
  We hope you will participate in the play.

_____

     (Sign here if you want to participate in the play and
return this tear-off sheet by April first.)

I _____ want to be
   (First name)   (Last name)

in the play The Lion, The Witch, and The Wardrobe. The

characters (or stage helpers, or both) I want to be are

_____
_____

Figure 4–3 Posted on the Help Wanted Board

years to finish? Problems like this come up a lot in a writer's life. Characters need names, plots need twists, and thick writing needs to be thinned out. Fellow writers can, and do, help each other sort through these problems, making suggestions and creating solutions. By developing our writing community in our classroom we allow our students to become less dependent on us and more interdependent on each other.

Ultimately, most published writers *are* independent, and do most of their work alone. In that way, there was some truth to my teenage-angst writing dreams. Our students will end up spending a majority of their writing time outside of school alone. But because writing is, by nature, such a solitary activity it is extremely important that we explicitly teach our students how to build and exist within a writing community. By emphasizing a writing community's importance in an independent writer's life, we help ensure our students get those non-solitary needs met.

Committing to a Writing Community

Tuesday nights at six o'clock I take the N train from Brooklyn to Manhattan. All my friends and family know I'm not around on Tuesdays. I have my writing workshop. We meet in our workshop leader's apartment near Washington Square Park. Every week we gather in Jennifer Belle's (author of *Going Down* and *High Maintenance*) living room around a coffee table, sip seltzer, and talk about our writing. At least that's what I imagine it might look like to a bystander. We do much more than that.

There is a core group of seven to ten writers in various stages of their writing careers. A few make their living solely through writing. Others write alongside their day jobs. We each bring anywhere from one to eight pages to read each week, mostly pieces from drafts of novels. Then we "workshop" the pieces. That might include making suggestions, offering critiques, or complimenting good work. We may recommend books to read, brainstorm titles, or argue over stylistic choices.

The writing workshop I belong to is more than a place to be criticized. It is a group of people that are traveling on almost the same road I am traveling on. They not only understand what I'm going through, they're going through it too. Both the quantity and the quality of my work grew as more and more time passed.

I belonged to my writing workshop for an entire year before I made the teaching connection: if this was helping *me* so much as a writer, then I should see if anything we were doing as adult writers could help my students. I decided to turn again to the study of my own writing life. I talked to the members of my workshop, my teaching colleagues, and my leadership group and then read everything I could find about adult writing workshops. What I realized is that when adult writers got together for a workshop, despite the many surface differences such as routines, a few things were at the heart of most workshops. Writing workshops in the adult world are places where writers:

- Meet regularly
- Criticize
- Compliment
- Offer advice, and
- Support each other.

It seemed to me that none of these traits from my own experiences with groups of writers were beyond of the abilities of my students. In fact, they were already doing much of the work already. I only needed to validate their instincts even further, and create more opportunities for explicit instruction on the topic.

Writers, like most artists, thrive when they are able occasionally to move out of their solitary work into a community of peers. These groups of writers go by different names: the workshop, the salon, and the colony.

As teachers, we strive to create a similar community atmosphere for our students in our classrooms, and especially in our writing workshops. There are many books that discuss the importance of building community with our students. When I compared what I learned about adult writing workshops with what I knew about building community in a classroom, however, I realized that when our students moved toward becoming more independent writers it was different.

What Is a Writing Colony?

It doesn't matter what you call it, writing colony, salon, or group. In my non-teaching life I call it "writing workshop. " For many teachers, "writing workshop" has come to mean a model of teaching and the chunk of time we use to get the teaching of writing done. It includes the mini-lesson, writing time, conferences, and the sharing of writing. For the sake of clarity I will use different terms to refer to different configurations of classroom community I am talking about. While these terms are by no means written in stone, I have found that looking at what adult writers do, we can find names that are already in the world for different kinds of writing communities.

For me the Writing Colony is the whole class, including the teacher. Just like a professional writer might take a month and go to a writing colony in Vermont where everyone dedicates time in the secluded woods to writing, everyone in my class dedicates part of their time to writing. By offering a community where every member is engaged in similar struggles, we offer our independent writers the knowledge that they are not alone.

In a classroom there is around twenty-five to thirty people in close proximity working on our writing. In an adult writing colony, we would never expect every writer to be constantly in close contact with every other writer. It's just not realistic. They need time to walk in the woods, time to stare out the window; time to write.

But there will probably be times at a writing colony when writers meet up, maybe over dinner, to discuss writing. These writers, anywhere from four to eight people, are more committed to each other. They may drift in and out of the group on occasion, but they are most often constant. This group is instrumental in guiding independent writers through their writing process. The group is large enough to offer the independent writer diversity of opinion but small enough to allow more timid voices to feel more secure. These folks I call the *salon,* thinking of those American expatriates in Paris during the 1920s and 30s. The salon is the configuration closest to the adult writing workshop model I attend.

Then, within the salon or from other meeting places, there are smaller clumps of people. They usually get together to focus on a topic or problem. The Teachers College Reading and Writing Project calls these writers a *writing club.* Other teachers call this configuration a writing group. These may be permanent groups, whose members might even co-author pieces. Independent writers often find writing clubs useful when they want to study a topic in depth and need support or are working on a large project and want co-writers. Or a writer may need to develop trust with fellow writers in a small group environment before feeling safe enough to have her work critiqued.

Finally, the last grouping I've observed can be either permanent or temporary. These are *writing partnerships,* couplings that may last for one five-minute share session or throughout the school year. These can be both teacher and student created. Writing partnerships offer the greatest level of intimacy since there are only two people involved. For many independent writers the support of a partner is a fairly nonthreatening alternative to larger groups. And an independent writer can build a strong understanding of one person's work and growth and enjoy a strong mutual bond. (See chart.) These are all reciprocal relationships: writers help each other because they are getting help as well.

WRITERS' GROUPS

Group	Number of Students	Length of time	Organized by
Writing Colony	Whole Class	Whole Year	Teacher
Salon	6–8	Permanent/Semi-Permanent	Students
Writing Club	3–5	1–8 weeks	Students
Partnership	Two	Varies from five minutes to a year	Teacher/ Student

Our Writing Colony

Teachers create their class writing colonies in different ways. In my class I made it very clear that I was as much a member of the colony as the students. I frequently shared my work, not just as a model, but also as a writer with joys and struggles. When I joined them on the rug in the circle with my writer's notebook in my lap, I sent my students a clear message about my status and the status of every member of our community. When it came to writing we were all in it together. I was as much a student of writing as they were.

I regularly gave students the first several minutes after the mini-lesson to talk to fellow writers, though I had not given an entire precious writing period to the practice. I decided to do just that one day in March when we were deep in the trenches of our realistic fiction study. I watched the students who had strong partnerships and clubs and they were (not surprisingly) having a much easier time wrestling with the challenging genre. I thought it would be great to offer that kind of support to everybody in the class, as well as reinforce the important role talk plays in the writing workshop.

During our next writing period I began by saying, "Okay, I noticed that some folks are feeling a little frustrated right about now. Which reminded me a lot of

Figure 4–4 Brainstorming Ideas with the Writing Colony

what I'm like when I'm in the big middle of a project. Some of you feel pretty good, but you could use some fresh eyes. I noticed a lot of you have been meeting with other people and getting help that way during our talk times. I thought today we could use the whole period just for talking." Some kids exchanged glances and made hand motions to the people they wanted to talk to during the period. Others looked nervous. *A whole period for just talking?*

Aidan asked, "But what if we finish talking before the period is over, can we go back to writing, or do we have to keep talking?"

"That's a good question. Because I want everyone to talk, whether you want to or not, I want you to have a conversation about your pieces for at least fifteen minutes. Then after that, if you have nothing left to say, you can go back to writing," I said.

"What are we supposed to talk about?" Oscar asked.

"That's another good question," I said. I talked about how the same types of things they had talked to their partners about earlier in the year would be a good jumping off point. I also said they might want to take this opportunity to trouble-shoot with what they might be struggling with. I posted a list for students to refer to while having their conversations. For students who have a difficult time referring to charts, I handed them a photocopied version they could tape in their notebooks:

Some Things Writers Talk to Each Other About
- Asking advice
- Giving advice
- Things that are going well
- Areas where they are stuck
- Plot ideas
- Character traits
- Confusing parts
- Compliments
- Worries
- Questions
- Word choice

After reviewing the list I fielded a few more questions, then sent them off to talk. The only rules were that they had to keep their voices down to a dull roar and they needed to talk about their realistic fiction pieces.

When I walked around the room I was once again impressed by what students will do when given an opportunity most adults take for granted—the chance to talk to each other. Ruthie, Nili, and Aaron gathered in a tight circle in front of the rocking chair. "I have so many questions for you guys. Like I know that I should have one major trouble in my story, but my story is so complicated I don't feel like

I can take any of the troubles out," Nili said. Ruthie and Aaron leaned in to look at her work.

Oscar and a friend sprawled out on the rug. Because writing longer pieces was a challenge for him, Oscar had spent a long time planning his piece. Now he flipped through his folder to find his drafts, "I'm not sure if this makes sense. What do you think?" he asked.

All around the room, conversations bounced and tumbled from topic to topic, writer to writer. Two of the quieter students in the class needed to be nudged to talk about their work and about other folks' writing, but they managed to get into the swing of things before too long. I sat on the edge of a table at one point to just drink it all in. Not one student was having a frivolous conversation or fooling around. Everywhere students were talking and listening to writing. I wanted to kick myself for all the times over the years that I felt that my students couldn't handle so much talk.

When we came back together as a group for our sharing session, students were abuzz with things to talk about. Eric said, "I am so happy now. I was completely stuck in my piece and I didn't even realize it until we started talking about it."

"I didn't think my piece was very good, but now I know other people like it," Kenya said.

It was unanimous; everyone wanted the opportunity to talk again during writing workshop. I knew my students had made a big step toward becoming better talkers. However, it wasn't until later in the year that I realized the simple act of giving them the space to talk and giving value to it had a ripple affect. The time for talking also helped pave the way for them to talk more often without teacher approval and thereby build a stronger writing colony.

Mini-Unit on Criticism

By the end of March my students actively worked on independent writing projects, using their mentors and notebooks to help, with very little direct teaching from me (since I was busy with our whole-class realistic fiction study curriculum at the time). I realized that peers would need to play a larger role in the writing process in order to give the students the support they needed. I thought a good place to shore up that support was through critique. I knew my students were *capable* of making thoughtful criticism, though they did not have a lot of experience with it. My students would need a very clear model of how that might look. I needed to put somebody's work (mine) on the chopping block so that they could see how peer criticism works and get some time to practice it. It would take more than one session for the students to get the hang of it, so I decided to string a few lessons together into a mini-unit on talking productively with other writers (that is, how to criticize effectively).

I started the mini-unit with a teacher-directed lesson, complete with a chart on ways to talk to another writer about his or her writing:

- Start with a sincere compliment.
- Be honest, but be kind.
- Make suggestions the writer can try right away.
- Use examples from other authors' work.

Although we had already spent a lot of time studying and practicing good writing conversations, we were going to another level and I wanted to feed them the information that would be new to many of my students.

The next day I began by saying, "I was looking at the latest draft of my independent feature article, and I think it's pretty good, but I could really use some fresh eyes. It's gotten to the point where I can't tell anymore what's good and what's garbage. Then I thought about my writing workshop and how the people in my group really help me make my novel so much better. I was thinking today, since you guys are such experts on feature articles, and we already talked yesterday about how to criticize writing well, you guys could be my writing workshop."

The students wiggled on the rug. They knew what I meant when I said they were going to be "my writing workshop. " They could hardly wait to get their chance to criticize me. I made sure to set up some ground rules. "Remember that we're trying to be helpful, not hurtful. So it really helps to start your comments with something positive before moving onto criticisms and suggestions. It can be hard to have other people judge your writing, so by keeping your comments positive, I'm more likely to listen to you. After all, it's up to the writer in the end to make decisions about her piece."

I put an overhead up of the article about cockroaches I had worked on with the class (Figure 4–5, 4–6). I passed out additional paper copies to students who had a difficult time tracking the action on the overhead. Because I had already done a lot of modeling using the piece, the students felt comfortable with it and also knew my intentions as a writer. I read the draft out-loud first. Then I stopped and looked at them. "So I have a lot of questions for you about this piece. There are definitely some areas that I think are weak and could use some help. But before I ask you about them, I want to know what you are thinking about."

There was silence at first. Not a long one, but long enough for me to reconsider whether I was right in thinking nine- and ten-year-olds were capable of criticism. Aaron, broke the silence. "I think it's good. It could go in a magazine like *Ranger Rick*. But you're right. It can definitely use more work."

"Thanks for your compliment. I could imagine it in *Ranger Rick* too. But, what do you think can use more work?" I asked.

Draft #2

Cockroaches: Indestructable Evil or Misunderstood Miracle Insect?

It is a quiet night in ~~a typical~~ your apartment. You stumble into your kitchen for a midnight snack. Blurry-eyed you flick on the light, only to discover -PURE HORROR! Everywhere, small many legged beasts scurry to and fro across your counters, your tiles, your butter dish. That's right, every midnight ~~snackers~~ worst nightmare - ~~the~~ cockroaches.

This is the ~~typical~~ opinion of 79% of the 25 people polled - cockroaches are more than a nuisance - they're a big problem. But is that entirely true?

The history of cockroaches

Long before human beings first set foot on this planet, approximately 400 million years ago, cockroaches joined earth's ecosystem. Classified in the Orthoptera order with crickets and grasshoppers, with 4000 - 7500 species of cockroaches

Figure 4–5 Draft of Cockroach Article the Students Criticized

on the planet they earned their own ~~family~~ separate order, the Blattoidea, family Blattida.

These hardy creatures have outlived millions of now extinct species such as the dinosaurs and the dodo bird. Despite human being's best efforts to rid themselves of the pests they stay ~~and~~ survive—and thrive.

Fast, ~~slick~~ smart and hardy

The cockroaches most commonly found in our homes (brought over on European ships from explorers and colonists 500 years ago) are the ~~Eu~~ American and German varieties.

It is these creatures unique bodies that help them to be fast (up to 6 miles per hour), smart (they can learn to navigate mazes) and hardy (they can survive for up to one month without their heads).

Their slick brown body has six

Figure 4–5 Continued

legs with 18 knees. Cockroaches also have beautiful transluscent wings that they only use when necessary.

Their slim ~~body~~ bodies can slip into crevices that are as small as the width of a quarter-1.46mm. Because they breathe through holes on the sides of their body called spiracles, they ~~ca~~ don't need their head to breathe. Also- they can hold their breath under water for 30-40 minutes. Because their brains are in their stomachs and they need very little food to survive, a cockroach does not need its head for at least 2 weeks before it will die (because of starvation).

Radiation, such as the proverbial nuclear war, won't kill but 1/4 of them because their cells divide so ~~fast~~ slow and only when they molt, ~~so ai~~ and radiation only attacks ~~moving~~ dividing cells.

Figure 4–5 Continued

COCKROACHES:
Indestructible Evil or Misunderstood Miracle Insect?

By Colleen Cruz

It is a quiet night in your apartment. You stumble into your kitchen for a midnight snack. Blurry-eyed, you flick on the light only to discover – PURE HORROR! Everywhere, small many legged beasts scurry to and fro across your counters, your stove, your butter dish. That's right, ever midnight snacker's worst nightmare – cockroaches.

At least that's the opinion of 79% of 25 people polled. Cockroaches are more than a nuisance. They're a big problem. But is that entirely true?

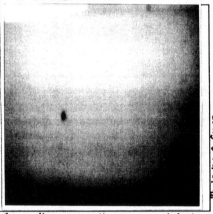

The results aren't pretty when a roach isn't wanted.

Older than dinosaurs, yet they live under your sink.

Long before human beings first set foot on this plant, approximately 340 million years ago, cockroaches joined the earth's **ecosystem**. Classified in the Orthoptera order with crickets and grasshoppers, with 4,000 – 7,500 species of cockroaches on Earth, they earned their own order, Blattoidea, family Blattida.

Surprisingly, these hardy creatures have outlived millions of now extinct species such as the wooly mammoth and the dodo bird. Despite humans' best efforts to rid themselves of the pests, they stay, survive and thrive.

As a matter of fact, cockroaches' natural habitat is the great outdoors, however as our human ancestors started to begin to live in caves and build primitive shelters, the cockroaches decided to move in. After all, the humans liked to store food in their homes, which made it a very easy life for a cockroach that once had to search through the forest for its dinner.

Fast, smart and hardy

The cockroaches most commonly found in our homes (brought over on European ships from explorers 500 years ago) are the American and German varieties.

The creatures unique body shape make

Figure 4–6 Final Piece, After Using Students' Criticisms to Help Revise

They stared at me blankly. I decided to prompt them a bit so they might see what, exactly, I was aiming for. "One thing I noticed is that my lead is pretty strong, but after that the piece gets a bit dragged down in all my cockroach facts. It almost sounds like a list. What do you think I should do about that?"

"Maybe you should put in an expert quote. That way it doesn't just sound like one person talking," offered Nili.

them fast (3.4 mph), smart (they can learn to navigate mazes) and hardy (they can survive for up to one month without their heads).

Their slick brown body has six legs, each with 3 knees (for you math wizards – that's 18 knees!). Cockroaches also have beautiful translucent wings that some use all the time, and other roaches never use.

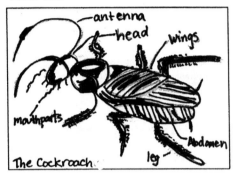

Their slim bodies can slip into crevices that are as small as the width of a quarter – 1.mm.

The insides of their bodies are just as incredible. They breathe through holes on the side of their bodies called **spiracles**. They don't need any pesky nose to breathe. That helps enable them to go without oxygen for up to 40 minutes – so there's no use trying to drown them!

A cockroach's heart is located in its **abdominal segment**. What's even stranger is that its blood doesn't flow through veins like ours does, but instead just sort of flows freely. It's because of this unusual **anatomy** that cockroach's are so hard to kill. When a cockroach loses its head, since its brain isn't in its head, and it breathes through its side, only way it will eventually die is by starving to death – which since a cockroach needs to little food may take a very long time!

Radiation, such as the proverbial nuclear war, would only kill one-fourth of the cockroach population. That's because radiation only kills rapidly dividing cells, and since cockroaches' cells only divide quickly when they **molt**, and they don't molt that often, well that means a lot of roaches would survive.

Yeah, but are they safe?

Despite how amazing their bodies are or how smart they might be, many people still find cockroaches disgusting. The number one reason? "I think they're dirty," says Kate Pollock 4th grade teacher and confirmed cockroach hater.

In fact, that's not true. Cockroaches clean their **antennae**, spines and legs all the time. And as for the belief that they carry diseases? "I'm afraid that's not true," says Wilford Cruz, former exterminator. "As much as I wish I could say they carry diseases – there just hasn't been any proof that they do. We do know that some people with asthma are allergic to them though."

Amazing Creatures . . . Now how do I get rid of them?

If you're still not convinced that the cockroach is a worthy creature and you want to raid your refrigerator without fear of unwanted guests, there are a few things that you can do.

- Make sure there's no food left out for them to eat. They'll go elsewhere.

- Leave the lights on. Cockroaches prefer the dark and rarely come out if there's lights on – unless they're overpopulated.

Figure 4–6 Continued

- Rub some oil or petroleum jelly around the mouth of a jar and put some food inside. Place the jar under the sink or any place else you know they visit. The cockroaches will climb in, but they won't be able to climb out.

- Spread Borax, a common household cleaner around your baseboards. It's pretty harmless to humans and the environment, but deadly to cockroaches.

- Buy some fans and open windows. Cockroaches don't like breezy places – it dries them out.

- Last resort – **pesticides**. These are dangerous to use if you have young children or pets and bad for the environment. However – they do take care of the problem – for now.

Keep in mind, however, that no matter what you do, you can't entirely rid yourself of cockroaches. The best you can hope for is that you'll *see* them less.

Cockroach Vocabulary:

abdominal segment: the middle part of the cockroach's body where its internal organs are.

anatomy: a creature's body, inside and out.

antennae: long tubes coming out of the cockroaches head that help it to sense temperature, motion and smell.

ecosystem: the complex system of life in a particular place, such as an aquarium, or a planet.

molt: when the cockroach sheds its skin – and sometimes a leg or two!

pesticide: a poison used to kill things that are annoying to humans.

spiracles: eight pairs of openings on each of the cockroaches side that allow it to take in air to breathe.

Figure 4–6 Continued

Ruthie jumped in, "Yeah, and since you do a really good job with describing the cockroaches, maybe you can also describe the setting a little more, like where they live."

"Wow, Nili and Ruthie, those are great ideas. I'm going to just jot those down right here in the margin so when I go to revise I can be sure to think about whether or not to try them," I said.

We went on like this for a few more minutes, the students jumping in to offer criticisms while I affirmed their good efforts and tweaked their not so good ones. I also made a point to talk as the writer and model ways writers might react to and use criticism from their peers.

Students went off with their writing partners to try out both roles. Walking around the room, I was pleased by their conversations. Students weren't just making the usual, "You need to use more descriptive language" and "You spelled that wrong" kinds of comments. They were digging deeply into each other's writing and having sophisticated dialogues.

On the third day, I complimented them on their work and then offered a few suggestions to stretch them even further. Had they considered how well their partner's piece was matching the genre? If their partner's piece was already good, what things would make it even better? Are there any bad writing habits you notice, such as weak verbs, too many "ing" words, or really long sentences?

It's worth repeating that it's invaluable for teachers to have samples of our own writing work to use as a model for our students. In this particular instance, it is extremely helpful to show the students what it is to criticize and also the attitude of the writer who is being criticized. Most students do not see this sort of conversation in their typical day-to-day lives. When creating a writing sample for this kind of work there are a few options to consider:

- While teaching an earlier unit of study, write alongside the students. The finished piece can be used again and again over the course of the year.
- One piece of writing can also be used in years to come if it fits into the unit of study and the unit's objectives.
- It's a good idea to share pieces of writing with colleagues. One teacher can write the feature article. Another can write the memoir. That way the workload is shared, and by talking about another author's work we are able to reinforce the idea that we, too, have a writing community.

If you decide to create a piece of writing specifically to be criticized it is helpful if it can exactly meet the needs of what you want your students to do. While it is tempting to make the piece sound very childlike and have lots of problems it's not a great idea. After all, we are also modeling good writing. When I write a piece I plan to use as a model for the students I try to use a good piece of writing as my mentor. I usually choose something written by adults for kids. When I wrote the cockroach article I chose a piece from *National Geographic for Kids* as my mentor. I did not pretend that my writing is worse than it is, or that I write like a ten-year-old. That would never have fooled them. Instead, I wrote the best I could in that genre of children's literature, though I did make a few planned mistakes that would make the students' work easier. When planning weakness to add to a piece I follow a few guidelines:

- *Use weaknesses you've noticed in your own students' work.* If my students forget to make paragraph breaks I do that. If they overuse certain vocabulary I do that. It's interesting to note how many of those writing tics will disappear when they spot it in their teacher's work.
- *Make sure there is one glaringly obvious mistake.* This is something I do not usually even have to do on purpose. I constantly misspell homophones. But if I

don't have one obvious mistake I add one. It helps students to see that everyone makes those kinds of mistakes, and also allows students who have a difficult time spotting things have a chance to succeed.

- *Make sure there is one very difficult-to-find mistake.* I put this one in for my smarty-pants like Aaron who swears he knows every correct grammar rule, phrasing choice, and stylistic option. It makes people like him work a little harder, as well as prove the art of criticism is not so simple.
- *Include weaknesses that you have included in your teaching.* If I spent ridiculous amounts of time making sure my ending was solid and supported my piece, then I need to make sure there is room for students to use that knowledge.
- *Remember to include weaknesses that are not about conventions.* Every weakness in the piece should not be spelling, grammar or punctuation. Areas such as clarity, meaning, flow of words, transitions, style and voice are more interesting and more realistic areas for there to be weaknesses.
- *Don't overdo it.* Inevitably students will find plenty more weaknesses than you intended. A few well-placed ones that leave plenty of room for good conversation are better than peppering a piece with problems so that students lose sight of the intention of the work.
- *Allow room to make the piece better.* Sometimes criticism is not about "fixing" a piece as much as it's about making a good piece better. It's good for students to realize that writers can make changes to an otherwise solid piece in order to make it fantastic.

This mini-unit and others like it are helpful when students are so involved in whole-class projects that they are barely working on their independent work. It offers them a chance to hone those community-building skills that will serve them well whenever they are working on independent projects and need to know how to get the help they need from other writers. The following chart is one possible way a mini-unit on criticism can go:

Day	Topic	Mini-lesson	Modifications	Possible Trouble
1	Criticism	Ways to talk to another writer about his/her writing	A check sheet that students who need more support can stick in their writing folder	
2	Criticism	Practicing criticizing and accepting criticism	See above	Some students can be mean-spirited. Other students can be sensitive. It's important to circulate throughout the class
3	Criticism	Further ways to criticize effectively	See above	See above

A Closer Look at Writing Groups

Writing Partnerships

Much has already been said by Calkins, Anderson, Ray and others about writing partnerships and their importance in the writing workshop. But however important they are in our whole-class writing workshop, they are doubly important when students are working on their independent projects.

When writing partnerships work well in whole-class studies, they often spill over into independent work. In many cases, students stay with the same writing partner throughout the school year. Some even find that they want to co-write pieces together. Others become book teams, like John Sczieska, writer, and Lane Smith, illustrator (*The Math Curse*).

Eric and Ruthie were a prime example of all the best a partnership has to offer. They were in the same salon together, though not usually in the same writing club. When there was partner talk to be had, it was understood that these two would be together. They criticized, suggested, and brainstormed freely with each other. Their relationship was so strong that they ultimately ended up publishing three pieces together. Their last piece, "Hoody," was inspired by a trip to the school library where they read *The Three Pigs* by David Wiesner. Eric and Ruthie used the story of "Little Red Riding Hood" as their bounce board.

Figure 4–7 Working Through the Tough Parts Together Is Part of a Good Partnership

When our students' partnerships work well we significantly cut down our workload. We can confer with partners. We know students are keeping themselves accountable so we're not as inclined to nag. Students are less needy when it comes to seeking approval, because that need is being met by their partner.

Over the years I have tried a variety of ways to pair off students. I have assigned partners according to interests or abilities. I have assigned partners according to their personalities. I have even had students chose a name out of a hat.

I allowed students to choose their own partners to work with on independent projects. I have found this worked the best when I gave the students a deadline and an ultimatum. I simply announced on a Monday, "Everyone in this class needs a writing partner. I trust that you can find your own partner who you work best with, but there are a few rules. Rule number one, I need everyone to have his or her partner chosen by Friday. Rule number two; everyone needs to have a partner. If there is anyone on Friday who does not have a partner I reserve the right to dissolve all the partnerships and create my own. In other words—don't leave people out. Rule number three, if there is a person who needs a partner and you would like him or her to join you; we can have a select few groups of three. Finally, I reserve the right to dissolve a partnership and move the partners if I think they will not work well together. So do not make the mistake of choosing somebody simply because she or he is your friend. Choose someone you can work with." I found that, although a little theatrical, this speech got the point across and I had very few partnership dilemmas.

Salons

Not every student is going to be a member of a salon. As a matter of fact, there may not be any people in your class in a salon. But for students who are particularly involved in their writing lives and, or, part of a very tightly knit class community, a salon is a natural progression. Certain students almost always form salons after the writing colony has been growing for a while. Usually their official formation comes after the teacher speaks briefly about the opportunity and what it entails.

One group of students was a great example of a salon. Eric, Ruthie, Aidan, Aaron, and Nili were all solid writing students and through various conversations with each other during share-times realized that they had a lot in common when it came to writing. They all loved to write, and the funnier the pieces the better. Writing was a big part of their personal lives and working on independent writing projects became one of their favorite things to do during their free time.

Since the students in my class had the option to talk to other writers during writing workshop, these five created their own way of balancing the workshop time. They would sit at the same table, work spread out in front of them. Sometimes they would begin by writing quietly. Eventually someone's head would pop up, "Guys, what do you think of this?" and the group would switch gears to listen and comment. Other days they would begin by picking up a conversation where they had left off from the day before. The first time I noticed them working like this I eavesdropped. I thought for sure that if they were talking *that much* they couldn't possibly be working on their writing. But when I listened in, I realized that they were doing exactly what many writing salons have always done—talking through the hard stuff in their work, sharing ideas, and inspiring each other.

Their shared relationship extended beyond whole-class studies. They ran proposals for independent projects by each other. They teamed up to create pieces. Their work as a salon soon leaked out to the rest of the colony. Eric became the "publisher" for Aidan's cookbook. He took Aidan's design ideas and used his home computer to generate a colorful layout for the cookbook. By the end of the school year Eric had served as "publisher" to several other students not in his group.

Salons offer students an opportunity to develop ongoing, close relationships with a group of writers. As I mentioned earlier, because of their size, dedication, and regularity, they most closely resemble the adult writing workshop. Salons are often jumping-off points for other relationships such as partnerships and clubs; however, I believe this particular configuration of students cannot be teacher-created. True, we have plenty of opportunities to manipulate our students' interactions with each other so that they get to know people we think would be good matches for them. But for a salon to really work it must come naturally from the students. Only writers who want to work and learn from each other will be able to make it through the long haul.

Writing Clubs

Sometimes kids in a salon periodically broke off into smaller groups to work on something more exclusive. When they formed that small group in order to study or make something together they had moved naturally into a writing club. Other times students who found they had a lot in common, or were struggling with similar issues, formed a writing club. Writing clubs, just like book clubs, are run by the members of the club. In my classroom, the major difference between the two is that unlike book clubs, every student does not end up in a writing club.

As I mentioned earlier, Aaron, Ruthie, and Nili made a connection during our whole-class talk session. The three went on to form a writing club during our class study of realistic fiction. They were drawn together because all three were interested in writing long and complex pieces, yet they needed support for the kind of work they wanted to do. Their supportive relationship was so vital to their writing lives that all three dedicated their finished writing pieces to each other. But when the study was over, the club dissolved back into the salon they were formerly members of.

Emily Smith a former fourth-grade teacher at P.S. 116, now a staff developer at the Teachers College Reading and Writing Project, has done a lot of work with

Figure 4–8a Eric took a fellow student's notes to "publish" her piece the way she wanted.

clubs. She said that while not every student was in a club, students who did choose to be in a club found them very helpful. Some of her clubs chose to meet during lunch periods in addition to writing time. Her clubs created a course of study for themselves, which meant anything from studying a mentor author to a genre they wanted to try. Emily felt that her responsibility to those clubs included

Figure 4–8b Eric's finished version of his fellow salon member's piece.

giving them time to work, seminars when needed, and supporting materials. Emily felt that one of the unexpected benefits of writing clubs was that most of the students who belonged to one were likely to carry their independent work over to the next school year because they had that built-in support.

I never seemed to have enough time to make clubs a formal part of my whole-class curriculum, though when I noticed students gravitating toward them I did take advantage of that teaching opportunity. Some things I taught to support club work were very similar to the kind of teaching we might do with our book clubs: listening, making thoughtful comments, and asking good questions. Members of writing clubs typically

- Give the writer what she or he needs by constructive criticism and supportive comments
- Ask good questions of the readers who are helping them so they can make the most out of their meeting

- Read a writer's work fully and deeply and offer comments as a *reader*
- Focus on the same topic/genre/challenge

The Seminar

I defined a seminar in my classroom as a sort of mini-lecture. An expert would talk to a small group of students for about twenty minutes on a given topic. Most of the time, since I was the "expert" giving the seminar, I made sure students had a hand-out to take with them to use as a reminder of the information covered. A seminar was not a time for discussion, but rather a time for students to soak in a lot of information at one time.

In my class seminars all followed a basic format. A seminar was a student-requested activity (or a teacher-hinted one). Around April, when other community structures were firmly in place, I had a class meeting to explain the seminar. Then I posted a sign-up sheet on the writing bulletin board. Students later signed up and listed the topics they wanted a seminar on. Sometimes writing clubs signed up together. Other times one student requested a seminar on a topic and when other students saw it listed, added their names to the sheet under that topic. Occasionally I listed a topic I thought folks might be interested in and left it up to the students to get excited or leave it alone. Students signed up for seminars on topics as varied as playwriting, comic books, notebook work, and the trials and tribulations of co-authoring a piece.

In my class, not all seminars were taught by me. Sometimes a teacher from another class, a parent, a student from another class, or even an expert from my own class taught a seminar. All that mattered was that the person who led the seminar was an expert on the topic and had a lot to teach other people about it. That said, I taught most of the seminars that took place in my class.

One April morning I taught a playwriting seminar to Kenya, Soroya, and two other students. The two partnerships had teamed up to request a seminar (I stipulated that there needed to be at least three and no more than six people interested for a seminar to take place). Kenya and Soroya had been working on their play since October and were beginning to panic as their planned deadline loomed. The other partnership was just curious about plays and thought they might want to try to write one.

The day before the seminar took place, I went through my files and books and found two examples of short plays we could look at together. I made some notes for myself so that I would be able to limit my talking to the twenty minutes I had allotted.

On Friday, after the whole class mini-lesson, the five of us gathered at a quiet table while everybody else went off to write. Then for the next twenty minutes, I gave a very teacher-directed lecture on the basics of playwriting: format, dialogue, stage directions, character development, and so on. The four girls took copious notes and hoarded the copies of plays I gave them. I left them enough time for questions at the end of our sessions before I went off to confer with the other students who had been writing.

Seminars give students an opportunity to choose what it is they want to study, just like a college student or a professional writer might. Granted, a seminar is basically a crash course in whatever subject is covered. But many students who are working on independent projects often choose to tackle things they have great excitement for but little experience with. A seminar gives them a jumping-off point for their learning, as well as a built-in community that they can study further with. Since I do so little straight-out knowledge dispensing in my regular teaching day, lecturing and sharing with students in such a small group, with such a hungry audience, is a thrill.

There are a few things to keep in mind when including seminars in a writing workshop:

- Seminars are student-chosen. Not every student will choose to do one. Although there are some similarities, this is *not* a guided writing session.
- Seminars are longer than a mini-lesson, but short enough to leave time to confer with other students during their writing work time.
- Students should leave a seminar with something in their hands: mentor texts, notes, and/or a handout with guidelines. In a seminar on newspapers, the students left with a copy of the local newspaper, a list of newspaper "do's and don'ts," and a blank dummy layout guide. By giving students something to take away we give them tools they will be able to build upon independently.
- Not all seminars are genre-based. Some are writing process–based, some are troubleshooting. It really just depends on the needs and interests of the students.
- It's fine to suggest a seminar if you notice a student might benefit from one. But ultimately it needs to be the student's idea to attend.
- Seminars are scheduled in advance. After a group signed up for a seminar I usually wrote a meeting date next to their request. I preferred to hold seminars on Fridays because that day has always felt a little looser to me. It also kept me from letting seminars take over my curriculum or, alternatively, get dropped.

Seminars offer students more autonomy in their learning, acknowledgment that they have their own writing agendas, and an opportunity to work with and support other students with similar interests. Of course there are no hard and fast rules for running a seminar. As always, the individual teacher knows best what will work well for her class.

For the Independent Writer, Community Is Vital

Isoke Nia often spoke about how important it was for students to use their classroom's resources while they were in the classroom. Many things, such as collecting in a notebook, can often be done at home, but other resources such as a teacher—and most importantly, their peers—are not available when our students leave for the day. More and more we need to impress upon our students that their community is invaluable in helping them grow as a writer.

It is sort of ironic that for our students (and many adult writers as well) to lead "independent" writing lives they need a community of writers available to support, advise, and criticize. Otherwise, those lofty goals for independent projects can be lost in the dust of frustration, loneliness, and an unrealistic reliance on the teacher.

Soroya and Kenya hung up a sign on their table, "We're writing. Do not disturb." They rattled marbles near their ears to capture the sound just right for their scary play. Eric had enjoyed the experience of publishing Aidan's work, so with help from his salon, he volunteered his computer and typing skills to a fellow writer. Word got around the class that Eric had a color printer and could make pieces look good. Kid-to-Kid publishing was born. Two other boys were so inspired by Oscar's comic books they created their own comic book, "Musky the Muskrat and Hunky the Hoboish Cat." The whole class waited with bated breath for the publication date after they saw the "Coming soon!" posters hanging in the hallway (Figure 4–9). The book was dog-eared within a week because the whole class had read it. These kids were members of a large supportive writing colony where everyone was working hard on their writing.

Exceptions

We all have at least one student for whom community is not crucial, and that can be a major source of annoyance for the student and the community as a whole. In my class, I have found that exposing that student to as many different communal experiences as possible is the path of least resistance. It's important that they get the opportunity to try out all of the configurations that exist in a class. But consistently forcing a student to work with other people when it is absolutely not her preference can lead to disastrous results. Entire clubs can dismantle, the unlucky partner can find himself trapped and unwanted, and the person who is stuck in a group when she would rather work by herself does very little writing.

These students will always be a member of the colony (whether they like it or not) and there is much to gain there. They will also have those temporary experiences that come from quick groupings and partnerships. Usually a student who likes to work alone works best in a partnership with someone with a similar working style. Of course, if after my best efforts the only community this writer regularly has

Figure 4–9 This "Coming Soon" sign drummed up a lot of enthusiasm for the partners' new comic book.

is the whole class and conferences with me, I don't push the issue. After all, it worked for J. D. Salinger.

Community-Building Mini-lessons

The following are some possible mini-lessons to teach while creating a colony. They can be taught as part of a mini-unit on community or added to another unit of study where they would make sense:

- *Why writers need other people.* Since most people write mostly by themselves, the various reasons writers need other people to help them might not be obvious to some students. It might be helpful to explicitly point out advantages such as: getting input and ideas, being less lonely, getting help with solving problems, etc.

- *How writers can help each other.* I offer a list of ways students can help each other in their writing. The list might include a range of simple to more complicated ideas such as:
  - offering a pencil to a writer who needs it
  - collaborating on a piece
  - making suggestions to make a good piece better
  - helping to find a good mentor text
  - encouraging each other
  - checking for spelling, grammar, and punctuation
- *Creating a strong writing colony.* This might include a study of what is working well in the class community, or it might be a study of what professional writers say about their communities. The students can then emulate those characteristics.
- *My responsibilities as a member of this colony.* This is particularly helpful for students who are not sure how they fit into the community or else have a difficult time being involved in positive ways. This mini-lesson can also be turned into a personal rubric where students assess whether or not they are kind, patient, helpful, come prepared to work, have a positive attitude, etc.
- *Making partnerships work.* This is an opportunity to offer strategies to students who might struggle with the finer points of work partnerships. Students might find studying a successful partnership and taking notes on their work helpful. They might also want to create a partnership rubric similar to the one mentioned above for being a member of the colony.
- *Making share time productive.* Those several minutes at the end of a mini-lesson are wonderful times to build community but, more importantly, they are teaching opportunities as well.
- *How to ask for and offer writing help.* This lesson can involve a variety of strategies for those important writing communications skills, which might include creating a class "Help Wanted/Help Offered" bulletin board, phrasing questions in positive ways, and asking for specific kinds of help.
- *Using human resources effectively.* The human resources are, of course, the classroom community. What are some ways to make sure we are taking full advantage of all the riches our classmates have to offer? This lesson connects nicely to the previous one.
- *Responsible criticism.* Learning how to criticize well and with kindness is a skill that takes some people years to master. It is important that students who are developing their independent writing skills learn this fine art so that they are able to be supported by and supportive of each other.
- *Hitting a writing plateau—how writing partners can help each other reach the next level.* Many of our strong writers produce volumes of good work, only to discover they have stalled. This lesson would talk about ways to shake up that sit-

uation by doing things such as trying new genres, working with a new partner, speed-writing, exploring an unknown topic, etc.

- *Co-writing: the fine art of working on a piece with another person.* This lesson would include why it is important to lay ground rules when working with another writer, what those ground rules might include, and reminders about positive interactions and criticisms.

5

Trouble!

Some teachers find September the most stressful time of year with its unknown variables and incessant lists of things to do. Other teachers dread the period surrounding test prep time with the additional pressure from the outside world combined with preparing students for tests without overwhelming them. Personally, I find May the most troublesome time. I feel the clock ticking ominously away with so much work to be done. Then there's my compulsion to review everything that I have not yet done during the year in order to undo or prevent any educational damage. I even have anxiety dreams during May.

In other words, I would read this chapter in May, the time when I feel as if I'm drowning in a sea of endless questions and problems. The wrinkles, slips and tears in our otherwise perfect plans for independent writing workshop will be addressed. I thought about the problems facing me while my students worked through the ups and downs of living independent writing lives. I also asked several other teachers from third through eighth grade to see what was most challenging or difficult for them when trying to foster a higher level of independence in their writing workshops.

I organized it by the most common concerns I had or had heard about this kind of work. Most of the troubles teachers encounter seem to fall into three major categories: management, quality of work, and meeting the needs of struggling writing students.

Management Trouble

How Can I Keep Track of My Students' Independent Work?

The task of guiding students through the process of writing when the entire class is studying one thing can be daunting enough. It is difficult to imagine, then, how one teacher can balance a whole room full of divergent projects. Even more frightening is when, later in the year, students are not only involved in a whole-class study, but are also regularly turning in independent pieces. What is an overworked teacher to do?

While I haven't found one magic solution, I have used a few structures to keep things a little more clear for the students and me. These structures can be introduced anytime during the year, however, I introduced them during my first unit on independence.

- *Proposal Sheet.* Students filled out a simple sheet, which listed the student's project topic, genre, deadline, and other important details. My students dropped the sheets into a basket on the writing shelf on a regular basis. I used the proposals as a sort of checkpoint where I could head off any obviously disastrous plans. The students knew they were approved when I returned the proposal to them stamped (I favored a stamp with Winnie the Pooh writing with pen and quill). I rarely rejected a proposal outright; instead I met with students with less than ideal proposals and we worked to revise the proposals together. Though there were few proposal rejections, when students received their "approved" proposal they responded very much like a professional writer receiving a green light from a publisher with excitement and a smile. On the reverse of the proposal was a small self-assessment the writer used when the piece was ready to be turned in (Figures 5–1 and 5–2). I also let students know that on occasion, if they were inspired to work on something and did not fill in the proposal sheet, I would be happy to accept it, as long as they still completed a self-assessment.
- *Class Deadline Calendar.* I hung a large calendar near the front of the room. When students received their approved proposal they were able to write their deadlines on the calendar. Most students simply put their initials next to the project. I was able to quickly check which deadlines were coming up or had passed. Another nice benefit was that students became more aware of each other's projects and would keep after each other to stick to the posted deadlines as well as feeling some good-natured peer pressure to produce more themselves (Figure 5–3).
- *Writing Process Chart.* This chart hangs prominently in many classrooms that have an ongoing writing workshop. The chart has different areas marked off for different steps in the writing process. Students are able to move their names (usually on magnets, or Velcro, or pushpins) along the chart as they move through the process. Some teachers use this chart as they move through each unit of study, so when the class is learning how to gather facts for a feature article, for example, everyone would have his or her name on the same step in the process. In my classroom this chart became a tool for me to keep track of my

---

WRITING PROPOSAL

Writer: _____   Date: _____

In the space below describe your project idea. Please be sure to include: **genre, what it's about (seed idea)**, and **expected publication date**, as well as anything else you might think would be useful to know.

_____

_____

_____

_____

_____

_____

_____
Writer's Signature

How did it go?

1. Did I write what I proposed?   ☐   ☐
                                         Yes   No

2. Did I publish by or before my deadline? ☐   ☐
                                         Yes   No

Comments? Reflections?

_____   _____
Kid's Signature   Date

Figure 5–1 The Front and Back of a Blank Proposal Sheet

Writing Proposal

Writer: _____   Date: November 2

In the space below describe your project idea. Please be sure to include: **genre**, what it's about (**seed idea**), and **expected publication date**, as well as anything else you might think would be useful to know.

I'm writing my second peice for this study. My new peice is a ~~poem book~~ non-fiction and I'm expeckting to be finished by November 13th and my next peice might connect to this one.

_____
Writer's Signature

How did it go?

1. Did I write what I proposed?   ■ Yes   ☐ No

2. Did I publish by or before my deadline?   ■ Yes   ☐ No

Comments? Reflections?:

This peice didn't seem to be to hard, because I love poetry and I'll almost an expert on poetry

_____   _____
Kid's Signature   Date

Figure 5–2 Proposal Sheets Filled Out by Students

Figure 5–3 Our Writing Deadline Calendar

independent writers only. I could easily look to see if Oscar was stuck on drafting for a while or if Aaron always skipped revision. I did not use the chart for whole-class studies since we were traveling through the process (for the most part) together.

I make sure students know that within each step of the process they can be reading and talking to support that step in addition to writing. So, for example, if Nili's magnet is in the "revision" box she could be meeting with another student to talk about possible revisions, rereading her mentor text to get some ideas, or actually writing down her changes on her draft. For some classes I have actually divided up the chart into three columns for each option: writing, reading, or talking. That way students not only let their magnets signify the step they are in but also let me know what kind of work I can expect to see them doing within that step.

Hey Writers! Where are you in the process?

Collecting: Living like a writer, writing in your writer's notebook, looking for good ideas, etc.	Nurturing: Choosing a topic to make a piece about (seed idea) and thinking about, talking about and writing in your notebook about it.	Drafting: Taking all your ideas and plans from nurturing, coming out of your notebook and creating a draft.
Oscar Ruthie	Kenya Libby	Felix Aidan Shaquanie
Revising: Looking at your draft with new eyes to make it better. Add, subtract, change, etc.	Editing: Checking for and changing spelling, grammar, punctuation, capitalization and awkward sentences.	Publishing: Finishing up your piece by making it ready for the world! Type or write in pen, decorate, illustrate and share it. Celebrate . . .now what are you going to do?
Lisa Aaron	Eric Amy Terry	Nili

Figure 5–4 Sample of a Writing Process Chart

How Do Students Keep Track of Their Own Work?

In addition to those whole class methods, there were a few individual strategies I taught students to use, which seemed to help them find that careful balance between independent and whole class work.

- *Idea Lists.* Some professional writers have idea notebooks or journals to keep track of ideas for future projects. While it would be great if each student could carry around his or her own idea notebook, that is not always practical. Every student in my class reserved the last page of his or her writer's notebook to jot down ideas for independent writing projects. That way, there were no lost ideas and no chance that students could say, "I'm done. Now what do I do?" As students finished a project they had the distinct pleasure of checking it off the list.

- *Independent Writing Calendars.* Some years I gave students photocopied calendars to keep in their writing folders; the year I co-taught in an inclusive classroom we created a homework organizer that contained a calendar. Students kept track of whole-class deadlines posted on the writing bulletin board in order to balance their own self-imposed deadlines. Ruthie liked to use different colored pens to differentiate between whole-class deadlines and her personal deadlines. The calendars also became places for students to plan out the pacing of a project. So when Letty worked on her picture book on dogs she blocked off three days to research dogs before she began to draft.

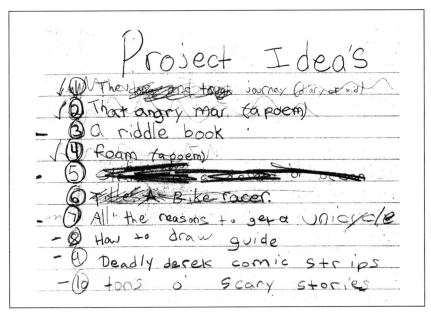

Figure 5–5 One Student's Project Ideas

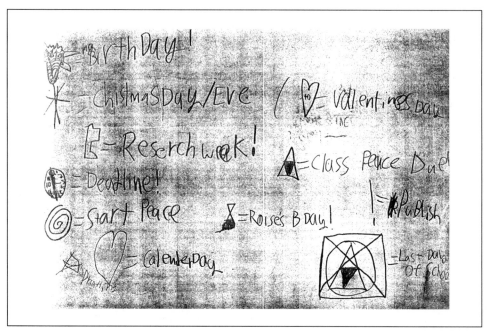

Figure 5–6 One Student Came Up with Her Own Code to Use with Her Calendar

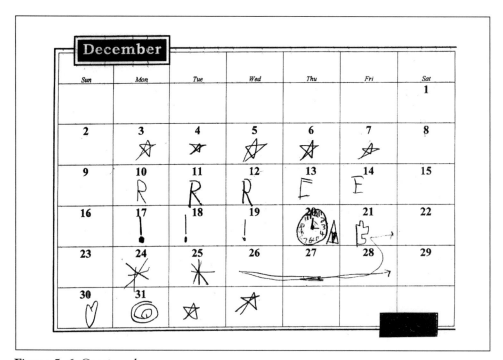

Figure 5–6 Continued

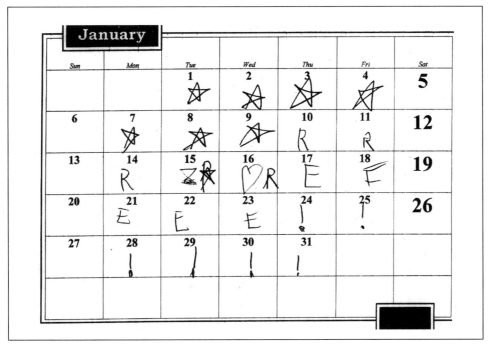

Figure 5–6 Continued

How Do I Grade All Those Published Pieces?

Depending on how prolific the class was, the act of reading and acknowledging each independent piece was plenty enough for me without having to be concerned about assigning a grade. After all, last year my class published ten pieces, which I definitely needed to spend time assessing. Besides, because my overarching goal was for my students to become lifelong independent writers, I did not want them to be writing solely for a grade. But I needed to balance that notion with the reality that students do need feedback, as well as to be held accountable for their work.

In the end I came up with a compromise that offered feedback and student accountability while also putting more assessment responsibility in the students' hands and saving myself grading time. I graded the first independently published piece with a rubric score (4 being the highest) and used that piece as a benchmark for the ones to come after it. Then I developed criteria for an overall "Independence" grade. Students were required to:

- Complete *at least* 3 pieces independently.
- Fill out a proposal sheet and self-assessment for a majority of the pieces.
- Write one piece from a genre we studied as a class.

- Write one piece that was going to go out in the world (a song, a letter, a sign, etc.).
- Follow class guidelines for publication: each piece needed to be written in pen or typed, checked for spelling, punctuation and grammar, and all drafts had to be attached.

Students were then assessed based on their entire body of independent work.

What Do I Do If My Students Write in Genres I Have No Experience With?

There are a few genres I have little or no experience with, in large part because I do not enjoy reading them. My two least favorite are comic books and science fiction. Comic books in particular, with their emphasis on illustration, not necessarily on written language, posed a particular problem. Interestingly enough, I have also found that my most reluctant writers tended to gravitate towards those genres. I have been tempted to tell my students that that sort of writing was banned from classroom publication in favor of a more literary variety. Yet I knew this completely went against my beliefs in the student's ultimate freedom to chart his or her independent writing course. I also realized that there were many respected professionals in those genres whose work was in fact considered literary—for example, Art Spiegelman's *Maus* and Arthur C. Clarke's *Childhood's End*. In fact, comic books, and their lengthier relative the graphic novel, with their combination of artwork and language, were actually a complicated genre. They allowed for a unique method of story telling which included all the story elements and required a writer-artist to coordinate a complex assortment of skills. Besides, I idolized Snoopy when I was a kid. I loved it when he dragged his typewriter on top of his doghouse and began to write his novel. He would type away, weaving imaginary worlds for himself with his words. A pretty good childhood model for the writing life, one might argue, was found inside a comic strip.

I decided to have conversation with the students who wanted to write in the genres I was unfamiliar with so they could educate me about them. Some of the students knew very little about the genre in question. If that turned out to be so, I sent them off to do some reading so that they became experts. Most of my independent writers who proposed something like science fiction were absolutely expert and were able to teach me quite a bit, as well as recommend a few examples for me to read.

If there was a group of students interested in a unique genre, they might request a seminar. As for science fiction, I had a student expert give the seminar, but I sat in on it. In the case of comic books, I felt as if I needed to do more since it was so popular. I spent a few days giving myself a crash course on comic book writing and even found a few books on how to create comic books. I added those books to our writing shelf as references for my comic book writers.

In general, I weighed the value of my knowing a genre really well versus being able to steer students in the direction where they could learn more (from other students, books written about the genre, etc.) on their own. The latter was actually the ideal situation, because it offered them yet another tool for leading independent writing lives outside of school.

How Do I Balance an Independent Writing Workshop with the Pressures of Standardized Testing?

Fourth-graders in New York City, as in most schools in the United States, take high stakes tests. The test results do not just reflect on the school, but in some cases can determine promotion to the next grade level and the ability to attend the middle school of the child's choice. Our reading and writing (ELA) test dates fell toward the end of January. That meant students were being tested in the middle of a time period when students were comfortably in the groove of fourth-grade life. I was concerned that there was going to be difficulty trying to balance preparing for the test with working on their independent projects.

Almost all of my literacy lessons during the month of January were aimed at helping the students prepare for the test, so most of our workshop time was spent studying the ELA test as a particular genre, and practicing writing in that genre. While students were learning a lot from this unit of study, it was not particularly being put to use outside of the confines of school.

I was pleasantly surprised after having taught during testing season for awhile. The students, and what they were capable of, did not change just because we had a big test to prepare for. I realized that as students lived their independent writing lives during this time, they did not feel creatively stifled when it got close to test crunch time and non-test writing lessons become a rare commodity.

Interesting, too, was that students' independent writing was thriving more than it had during other units of study. Students found that because preparing for the test was so classroom specific they had more time to work on their independent writing at home and during free time. January had become one time, other than the summer months, when students were able to prove their independent mettle because I was less available to confer, offer seminars, or support them in any formal way with their projects.

Additionally, I found that my students' experiences with their independent writing was an unplanned-for boon in preparing them for the tests. They had been exposed to more genres than I normally would have had time to cover because their independent writing diet was so varied. They also had a rigor to their writing life that meant they were writing consistently and practicing their writing skills, which made some of the length of the test and its expectations in terms of mechanics and the like seem less daunting.

How Do I Fit Independent Writing into My Already Overcrowded Curriculum?

The first thing I noticed when I began teaching independence a few years ago was how much it helped with classroom management. I had once feared it would be a managing nightmare but, quite the contrary, it made my management far smoother. Before independence became a regular part of my yearly curriculum, fast writers like Ruthie might have written meaningless entries in her writer's notebook when she finished the work introduced in the day's mini-lesson, while students like Aidan would daydream about sports after he finished drafting and waited to be taught about the latest revision techniques. I often noticed struggling writers who needed my help before they could move on in their work doodling in their notebooks while waiting for me to free up for a conference. After my students were introduced to the concept of independence, they were more likely to be *writing* during workshop. They had fewer excuses and, more important, less desire to be off-task.

One day during a whole-class study of revision techniques, after a brief mini-lesson examining the importance of structure, students tried the new techniques on their drafts. For several students for whom structure was not an issue, it took about five to ten minutes to "have a go." Then, without me corralling them into working, the students moved off to their own work. It was amazing to me how smooth the transition was. They simply slipped from the revision study to their own projects. Students flipped to the back of their notebooks where their "Future Projects" lists were or to their calendars to see what they had scheduled. They moved their name magnets on the writing process chart to reflect where they were. They borrowed highlighters and post-its from the silver shelf.

The rest of the period was a buzz of concentrated activity. While my first few conferences were usually about the mini-lesson I had just taught, many of my other conferences were about the students' independent work. We talked about where they got stuck (usually because they hadn't nurtured their seed idea enough), where they needed extra support (usually the particulars of an untried genre) and where they needed to be pushed to the next level (the actual published pieces were sometimes rushed).

That day was not isolated. We developed a pattern to our writing workshop from that point on. I would teach a mini-lesson. The students would apply the mini-lesson or opt not to. Then Ruthie would return to her Magic Crayon series and Aidan to plotting out the next scene in his new science fiction short story. Some days there was no time for independent projects within the confines of our work time. Other days there was much more time. Students took to cheering when I made the announcement during morning meeting that we would have an extra long chunk of writing time that day. They knew what a gift that was.

Writing Quality

How Do I Make Sure that My Students' Independent Writing Is the Same High Quality as the Pieces They Create from Whole Class Studies?

The short answer is: you can't. At least, at first.

For many of us who experimented with building an independent workshop in our classrooms, it was this quandary that seemed to bother us the most. I for instance, was used to working with students for weeks on the finer points of craft, content, and presentation during whole-class studies. The pieces that resulted varied from good to excellent. When my students began to publish their independent projects I was appalled. The pieces were more often than not messily written. The students, freed from the teacher-controlled pace of moving through the process of writing, often skipped important steps or rushed through to the exciting drafting parts. Some students skipped revision all together and claimed that they finished a piece after only one draft. And there were pieces missing elements we had studied over and over again. "There's no lead in this piece. Where's the lead?" I yelped. What had happened to my excellent writers?

Some may argue that students needed a teacher nudging them toward their capabilities, so the lack of quality is an indicator that students in the elementary grades are not ready to publish independently. Others will say it's just a sign of laziness—the students really could do better but just don't feel like it. Since I know that students can, and do, publish good quality independent pieces, and I don't believe laziness is ever the root cause of anything, I had to come up with other explanations.

First of all, I believe that we all need an audience when we write. When we have an audience we want to impress, our writing improves exponentially. (Case in point: compare the writing from your postcards to family with a speech to colleagues.) By simply creating a place in the room to display recently published independent pieces students were more prone to increase the level of quality. I also brainstormed with the students different ways we could publish our work:

- Mail it to a friend or relative.
- Write it on a t-shirt.
- Make photocopies and pass them out.
- Make a sign or poster out of the piece and hang it on a lamp post.
- Get a bunch of friends' pieces together and make an anthology.

Once students started to see other possibilities beyond the teacher's eyes, the enthusiasm for improving the work as a whole grew.

Secondly, many kids are trying out genres for the first time. Most of the students will publish at least one piece in a genre they have never been taught in school. Though Aidan might have vaguely remembered that lesson on the value of realistic dialogue, he was more concerned with what to name his head robot in his science fiction story and how to make the time traveling space ship sound cool. Mel Levine, author of *All Kinds of Minds*, observe that writing is one of the most challenging activities for student(s) because there are so many variables to deal with: letter formation, sentence structure, spelling, and the like. Now throw in the finer points of genre and it's a wonder the words are even in some semblance of order. One way to combat this tendency is to make sure seminars are readily available to all students.

Third, some students are impatient to be finished and rush through the process, even when they should be taking more time with certain steps. This tendency to rush comes from a variety of causes. Some students are nervous to be judged solely on their own merits. The ability to blame their less than stellar work on not understanding something in class, or another student bothering them, is taken away when students write independently. By rushing, a student has a new excuse in his or her back pocket in case a piece is not well-received. Other students are overwhelmed by the possibilities of writing everything on their "to do" list and want to hurry to get to everything. Then there are the students who simply have not internalized the process enough to see why writers must do a variety of things to make a piece. It is helpful for all students to have an open dialogue about the tendency to rush and the reasons one might feel tempted. Often that dialogue is enough to slow most students down (no one wants to be seen as insecure, after all). And going through the process of writing and why so many different components are involved will help students see the value of taking the time to make the most of the journey.

Finally, as painful as it can sometimes be to admit, independence is the ultimate form of writing assessment (see Chapter 6) for both student and teacher. If a student is not using sensory details when details are needed, it is probably because, even though the student was introduced to them, she or he has not yet internalized that skill. By making self-assessment and peer assessment a regular part of an independent workshop, students will soon see what they need additional help in. What's more, because independent writers are so motivated, it's more than likely the student will seek out the teacher for help.

For me, I found independently published pieces a fabulous barometer to indicate how well my class was mastering the lessons I taught. When I read through their pieces I looked to see what was being done well and what was lacking. Then I planned my lessons in my next unit of study accordingly. One year, after reading six pieces from different genres none of which ever mentioned time passing, I knew I had to change my plans to include more direct teaching on that important story element.

The scariest thing for some of us is giving up our jobs with quality control. We like to make sure that everything that comes out of our classroom is the best it can

Figure 5–7 This student is taking a survey for his independent writing piece—a strategy he learned during the class feature article study earlier in the year.

be. The key to feeling comfortable about the quality of independent pieces is to remember it *is* the best it can possibly be as an independent piece. Just the fact that the students are able to move themselves independently through the writing process is evidence of very high quality work. It is also important to remember that the more the students publish independently the better the pieces become.

I have never had a class where every independent piece was just as good as the ones published with the whole class. But I have seen the best pieces of the year, and the most highly acclaimed within the classroom community, come from independent writing.

Are There Other Ways to Raise the Quality of Independent Writing?

Beyond the ways already mentioned, a few others are worth trying. Sometimes I have used all of these methods, other years just one or two. As with every other teaching decision, when trying to raise the level of students' work it is up to the teacher to decide what best fits her students' need.

PUSH MENTORS The more students use mentors the better the pieces become. Knowing this, I am amazed at how many of my students, despite the fact that we have studied mentors formally and informally throughout the year, despite the fact the students have had success using them, and despite the fact that I talk about mentors every free chance I get, still do not have the instinct to use a mentor when working on a piece of writing.

I find that the only way to make the act of choosing and using a mentor throughout the writing process instinctive for my students is to really push it on them. By push it, I mean, there are certain students who become so sick of me plopping down next to them, a file folder filled with possible mentors in my hands, that they eventually learn to always have a mentor at the ready. By nudging our students to check with a mentor text when they have questions about writing be it craft, punctuation, or even layout on the page, they start to internalize the habits of more established writers and raise the level of their work.

DEVELOP PERSONAL RUBRICS Some teachers have students give themselves a rubric score for each independently published piece. This rubric score can be as simple as a number system that corresponds to the school's standards or a rubric score that the student creates for himself. On occasion I have asked students to simply jot on a sticky note a score they gave themselves (4 is the highest score in our class) and a one-sentence explanation for that score. Many students end up assessing their work quite honestly and strive to do better based on their own standards—which is my ultimate goal for an independent writer's assessment.

STUDY REVISION When there is a whole-class study on revision, many students choose an independent piece as one of the pieces to revise. By seeing the improvement in the piece, many students are able to internalize on their own what they are capable of. I like to teach a short unit in revision about midway through the year, at about the time many of my students have become a little cocky—since they are so much closer to being fifth graders than fourth graders. It is powerful for students to look at pieces with eyes focused on revision. They frequently discover personal bad writing habits, common mistakes, and sloppy work. They also discover where their strengths are and can use those strengths to shore up the weaknesses.

It's a good idea to teach students a variety of revision techniques such as adding dialogue, starting the story at a different point, removing unnecessary details, and so on. That way they can choose the technique that works best for them and are more likely to apply it to their independent work.

CONFER MORE The more I was able to meet with students about their independent work the better it became. It is very easy to let the number of students we confer with in a day shrink as we have other things to do during a writing period, such as giving a seminar, or meeting with a writing club. But even when students are having success in their independent work they still need the assistance of an outside, more experienced eye.

Figure 5–8 A student revises her work with an eye toward word choice.

I've found that when students work as independent writers, the role of the teacher in a conference becomes more like that of an editor. A teacher has the final say in most schoolwork and can use a variety of techniques to get the level of work that she wants from her students. An editor is more often part of the writing team. While the writer does the actual putting words to paper, the editor is a guide and advise to best express the writer's intentions.

When I meet with a writer working on an independent piece, I am more interested in helping the student meet her goals for that piece than I am in making it conform to my standards. But I have also noticed that the more I meet with students in that capacity, the more likely they are to write higher quality pieces, just as professional writers who meet regularly with their editors do.

REVISIT INDEPENDENCE AS A MINI-UNIT We took one valuable school week to evaluate our writing past and plan for our writing future. We caught our breath from our whole-class study, and made connections between our independent work and our class work. Then we checked to make sure everyone was on track.

After time and practice over the course of the school year, students had developed the skills and discipline to successfully balance two writing pieces: their assigned class work and their independent work. It never ceased to amaze me that so much time was used efficiently in the writer's workshop once independence was established.

When students finished with one task they moved on to the next. There was very little down time. Because every second of writing time was being used in some way, in April I found myself in the typical predicament of teachers everywhere—the more the students were doing, the less time we had. Taking Isoke Nia's advice, I created a new timesaving rule in my classroom: all general notebook writing should be done at home. By spring of fourth grade my students knew what was expected of their notebooks and with very few exceptions could do most daily notebook writing outside of school.

As usual, I took extreme measures. One day I announced, "From now on, unless there is some in-class assignment, extreme inspiration, or major nurturing going on, I don't want to see any more everyday notebook entry writing. You know you can do that outside of school. Instead, I want you to go on to whatever your next step is for you. I want you to do the stuff in class that you can do best in class."

At first there was the usual mutinous grumblings, but my students soon saw that they now had more time to best make use of the resources offered by their peers and classroom. This freed up more time for students to draft and talk to their fellow writers, and it gave me the ability to see what a student was really working on other than, "I'm just writing another entry in my notebook." When students were expected to always be in the act of creating something with their writing the rigor goes up, but so does the interest. After all, we became a class that produced stuff. With the increased production student mentors abounded and the peer pressure to care about writing intensified. Even the most unmotivated writers could find *something* they were dying to write about.

We also checked to see how our plans were going. Had we added to our list of projects? Were we sticking to deadlines? Did we remember to refer to our calendars? I met with several different groups of students to do quick-fix seminars based on observations and discussions.

This "check-up" was different every year. One year I spent more time on whole-class editing lessons and focused on nurturing in small groups and conferences. The next year I discovered that neither of those topics needed to be taught. That class needed more work on revision.

Touching base with my students at least once midyear, specifically regarding the independent workshop, allowed me to troubleshoot, assess, and plan for the remainder of the year while also raising the level of quality.

Meeting the Needs of Struggling Writing Students

How Will I Get Students Who Say They Hate Writing to Publish Independently?

Every year there are at least a few children (if not many more) who announce, "I hate writing!" Trying to get the students to fulfill a barebones writing curriculum would be enough of a challenge without even thinking about these students working on independent projects. I'm not referring to kids who have such a difficult time writing that it has become a chore (see "How do I help student's with learning issues?" below). Instead I am referring to those students who would rather do just about anything than write.

I thought for sure Aaron would be just such a case. He was a very bright student who always received very high grades. So it was a bit of a surprise when I told the class on the first day of school how much I loved writing to hear Aaron mutter, "That's too bad because I despise it." I assumed that he was one of those students who excelled at every other subject, but struggled with writing.

When we finished our first unit of study, I was even more perplexed to discover that Aaron was an excellent writer. He had a wonderful vocabulary and great crafting technique. When I talked to him about his feelings he said simply, "I just think it's boring. I have better things to do." So by the time we were deep into the school year and students were producing independent pieces alongside whole class ones, I had few expectations for Aaron's work. What I noticed, though, was that his required pieces continued to be solid and his independent writing stretched and grew by leaps and bounds.

On the day he turned in a proposal for a novel, I knew I needed to talk to him to make sense of what I saw as a paradox. "It's simple, when I'm doing my independent work I can do whatever I want. The other writing is all stuff you want me to do." Aaron was not alone in his feelings. Over the year I have been amazed at how many students who claim to hate writing are actually talking about the set school curriculum, not the actual act of writing. Independence gives those students the room to find their own writing niche, as well as a reason to learn more about writing. I've also found that once students know they are free to write anything they want in their independent work, they are more likely to allow themselves to be open about whole-class studies.

Not all students who hate writing are like Aaron though. Some of them hate writing in the way I hate Swiss chard. I just don't like it, and no amount of trying it is going to make me like it. I try to meet those students halfway by finding another love of theirs. Can they make a poster? A how-to book? Jeffrey loved skateboarding so he decided to work on a guide for new skaters on how to do tricks. For those whose heels are so dug in there is no halfway, I offer the Swiss chard strategy, "You still have to do it. You may not like it, but it's good for you."

How Do I Help Students with Learning Issues?

In my roles as teacher of a general education class and as a co-teacher in an inclusive setting, I have seen a variety of learning issues that affect writing. They have ranged from the extreme (unable to hold the pencil long enough to form words) to the mild (gets confused with homophones).

I have found that many students who had a difficult time when faced with a whole-class writing project excelled when it came to independent projects. Perhaps it was because the students felt less pressure to meet teacher-created standards. Perhaps it was because many of these students chose genres that were rarely taught in school such as rap, comic books, and picture books. Perhaps it was just the overall excitement of planning and executing a piece by oneself. In any event, many students who I had had to haunt before they would turn in an assigned piece, regularly met deadlines they set for themselves.

There are still students however, for whom independent writing is as difficult as other writing. Because there are so many ways a student can struggle with writing, there are no one-size-fits-all answers for how to help. The best thing to do is to get to know the students well, and fast. If the student has an Individualized Education Plan (IEP), use it as a tool. Ask former teachers where the student had success. Talk to the child's family to gain insight. That way the independent workshop can be modified to make it work for the student. My former co-teacher, Jenifer Taets, said something about modifications for any subject that I found particularly apropos for writing; "We know the modifications are working when students are able to work independently. If they need us there the whole time, then we haven't done our job." The following are some strategies I have tried in order to allow my students to become as independent as possible in writing.

ORGANIZATION OF MATERIALS While there are myriad ways for students to be disorganized, I have most often experienced two kinds, which are in some ways conflicting: the student who loses things constantly and so regularly misplaces work, and the student who has so many possessions that he or he struggles to find the proper things at the proper time.

Oscar was the kind of student who had an almost empty cubby because he had misplaced everything from his math book to his homework folder. While the classroom was organized so that there was a certain place for everything, Oscar's things were frequently every place they shouldn't be. His reading notebook was found on the floor of the coat closet. I found his social studies log on my desk chair.

The strategy I worked out with Oscar required his input. We talked honestly about his trouble with organization and came up with a plan of action. Since Oscar lost three writer's notebooks from September to December we decided Oscar needed to have at least two different writer's notebooks, so that he would always have something he could use. Oscar came up with the plan to ask me to photocopy his first draft of a piece as soon as it was done so that if he lost it he wouldn't have to start over from scratch. While Oscar continued to lose things during the year the losses were no longer catastrophic because he had a backup system that kept his independent writing from coming to a screeching halt.

Lara's cubby was filled to overflowing by all of her overstuffed folders, books, and loose pieces of paper. Lara never threw anything out because she was afraid she might need it later. My teaching partner, Jenifer, had a conversation with Lara similar to mine with Oscar, as they discussed the trouble Lara seemed to be having keeping organized. Together they cleaned out Lara's cubby and book bag.

After they took stock of everything she had they formed a plan. Lara decided she wanted to keep everything in one place. So we all consolidated. It was too difficult for her to carry her homework folder back and forth to school as well as her writing folder; something was bound to get mixed up. She designated the left side of her folder for writing work and the right side of her folder for all other homework. She got rid of any extra writing notebooks, and instead divided up one notebook so there was room for both whole-class projects and independent ones.

ORGANIZATION OF IDEAS Some students have an overabundance of fabulous ideas and will talk your ear off with their stories and plans. But when they sit down and begin to draft, what was once clear becomes garbled when it hits the paper, or else they moan, "I don't know where to start." I have found it helpful for these students to spend more time nurturing their ideas through the planning process before going on to drafting.

I like to introduce several possible planning methods and have the student chose the one that fits best. The key for many students is to have options. Not every student thinks linearly so there should be at least one planning method that is not linear. Some students think visually, so a diagram or chart should be an option as well. My most common assortment of planning techniques include:

- *Planning boxes.* Many teachers have students line up from three to seven boxes vertically. Students can then put a phrase or sentence in each box describing what will happen in that section of the piece. It is a useful tool for students who need a visual planning strategy (Figure 5–9a).
- *Web.* For students who simply need to get their ideas down and organized around a central point as opposed to a particular sequence, a web is a helpful planning tool. It is especially helpful when writing pieces with nonnarrative structures (Figure 5–9b).
- *Flow Chart.* This planning method is similar to planning boxes in that writers can write brief notes about what will happen in each segment or scene. The boxes are not organized in a vertical manner but are instead connected by arrows. This is helpful for a student who finds it difficult to grasp forward motion in a piece.
- *Storyboards.* This planning method is popular with filmmakers and theater directors. It involves making a brief sketch of each scene (for film it's each

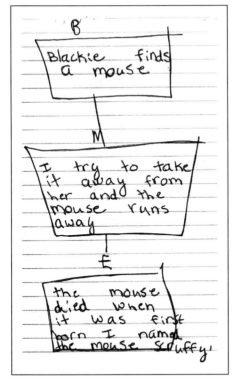

Figure 5–9a Planning Boxes

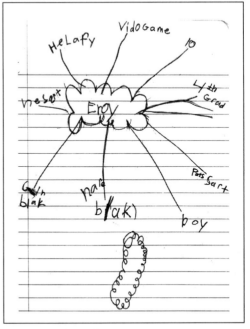

Figure 5–9b Web

shot) with the pictures organized to tell the story. This method works well for students who more visually oriented and might have a difficult time with words but are able to express more with pictures. Students who are allowed to plan by using pictures and a few words are often less reluctant to see drafting as an additional burden (Figure 5–9c).

- *Outline.* This traditional planning method allows students who have a difficult time seeing the organization of a piece into larger and smaller topics. It is particularly useful for students who still struggle with paragraph organization since the outline can be set up to support topic sentences and supporting details. This method is also helpful for students who need a very predictable and structured plan.
- *List.* This simple planning method can be used with fiction or nonfiction. It allows the writer to list in numerical order the way she envisions her piece going.
- *Timeline.* Timelines work best for pieces that have a chronological structure. Students who have difficulties with organizing chronology may find this help-

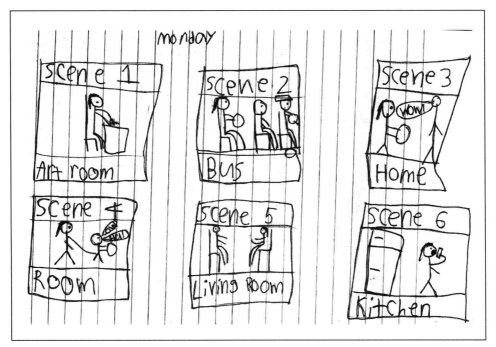

Figure 5–9c Storyboard

ful. The timeline begins at the start of the story and ends with the end of the story. The timeline can cover as much or as little time as the story needs. It is sometimes helpful to mark the halfway point for the writer, who can be asked to decide what will go in the beginning, middle, and end before deciding where the other events will fall.

- *Subtopics.* For students working on feature articles or other similarly organized nonfiction, creating a list of subtopics with the facts they have gathered is a helpful strategy. I have found it helpful to have the writer write each subtopic on a different index card. The student can then physically manipulate the well-written subtopic without hand-copying until the order makes sense. Then the student only has to fill in the paragraphs that make sense under each subtopic before filling in the facts and making a final draft.

RESOURCES When I co-taught in an inclusive setting we had a fairly high number of students for whom homework was a constant battle. Writing was a particularly difficult assignment to complete at home. When Jenifer and I talked to these students about what was happening, most of them shrugged their shoulders. When we asked specifics such as, "Where do you do your homework?" What supplies do you use?" "Who helps you with your homework?" and "When do you do your homework?" we learned that for most of our students who did not turn in home-work it was a matter of resources, not of will.

We worked out a homework plan for many of them, which included visualiz-ing a quiet place to work, choosing a regular time to work, and a phone list of classmate's numbers who would be helpful if the work got confusing. While those things might be taken for granted by some students, other students needed to be explicitly taught.

We also realized that in many homes there was a significant lack of paper and pencil resources. We made a homework package for a few of our students who needed those resources which included new notebooks, sticky notes, a few pens, a package of pencils with a small sharpener, markers, and a pack of looseleaf paper. The newness of school supplies and the excitement it brings can never be over-rated! We also let students know we had a ready supply of paper, pencils, and even writers' notebooks that could be used without asking. Since students knew these supplies were precious commodities, few abused the privilege. We found that after these resources were in place students were more likely to complete all their homework. Independent writing followed suit.

THE PHYSICAL ACT OF WRITING Every year I have a student for whom the mere act of holding a pencil in a recognizable grip is a Herculean effort. The fact that the student needs support from an occupational therapist or perhaps an eye specialist does not necessarily help with the day-to-day struggles of writing. The following list of strategies includes some I have tried as well as some my colleagues have found successful.

- *Access to a computer.* Many students who have a difficult time holding a pencil can learn to touch-type and thus be able to write with more efficiency. If you are lucky enough to have a computer in the classroom you might have the stu-dent who has such a problem doing everything from "notebook" writing to drafting using the keyboard. In a classroom where there is open dialogue about learning styles other students are unlikely to make a big deal about the accom-modation.
- *Sketching.* One student with a strong spelling disability but a strength in oral language and sketching developed his own way to keep his notebook and drafts. By combining words and pictures to organize his thoughts, he was able to "read" his work enough to either type it up or read it to an adult to type.
- *Dictation.* Using a tape recorder instead of a live human being to get ideas down is something countless writers have done for years. Making a tape recorder available to a student to take home enables the student to work independently to draft a piece, they can even replay the work and revise it on the same tape.

- *Buddy system.* Working with another student to write a piece is a common choice for struggling writers who are working on independent projects. The built-in support makes writing a significantly less daunting task.

For these and many other stumbling blocks, it is crucial to keep an open dialogue with the students. When we talk to our students about the trouble we notice they are having as well as their strengths they are more likely to be receptive and to become a partner in their learning and growth.

6

Taking Stock and Moving Forward: Assessment and Planning Writing Lives

By the time the end of the year rolled around, I felt an intense hodge-podge of emotions that had me feeling alternately celebratory and worried—celebratory because I knew my students had matured and stretched in ways I never could have imagined ten months before., worried because I found myself making the same mental checklist of "could've . . . should've." I could have given them more support in connecting particular genres to independent work, I should have taught more standardized grammar.

Before I got too lost in my self-flagellation, there were still a few things I wanted to accomplish in the weeks left with the students. I wanted to make sure their writing community was firmly in place so they would have people to talk to during the summer months. I wanted to assess the year as a whole and determine how they had grown and what new goals were left to be set. I wanted to set aside time to celebrate the success of our endeavors. Finally, I wanted to ensure that the students left me with a clear sense of their future writing plans.

The Home Stretch

I find that in the last few months of school, students always naturally feel more independent. I've tried to build on those independent leanings by using student attitudes to my own advantage for teaching.

June is also the time of year where I formally introduced writing clubs to students who hadn't already found them on their own. The clubs could be a powerful tool for students to use even through the summer months.

Though by this point many students had already attended a seminar, most students had not. June was a good time to remind them of the option to sign up for one. The seminar offered students the opportunity to collect as much information as possible in a short amount of time on sophisticated topics—information they could carry with them when they left. During the last weeks of the year, many students stretched their independent writing legs in new directions and a seminar often offered just the right amount of assistance.

Assessment

The kind of assessment that took place at the end of the year allowed me to take a more objective look at the year as a whole. I wanted to look closely at where my teaching had succeeded and where it was sorely lacking. I also wanted to study what each student had accomplished across the year, and I only was able to afford this luxury of time in June.

Not only did I need to assess, but so did the students. There is a pleasure that comes from looking over a body of work and studying one's own accomplishments. I wanted to give my students that opportunity to feel writing self-satisfaction. Once we had seen our accomplishments clearly, we would be ready to make our plans for future writing goals.

Assessing Ourselves

During a lunchtime planning meeting, Carl Anderson, staff developer and author of *How's It Going?*, said in one sentence something I believed was one of the central reasons teachers should teach students how to live independent writing lives. He said that when our students publish their writing independently, away from a whole-class study, the work they produce is the best means of assessing what they know about writing.

When we hold their hands and guide them through every step of a study, be it a genre study or a study in craft, the published pieces do not indicate what the students have learned and internalized about writing. It is only when they go through the writing process themselves, without our ever-present hands to guide them, that we can truly see what they have mastered. So in essence, each time we read another one of their independent pieces we are getting more pieces of the puzzle that reveals how much our students really know.

I talked to my colleague Kate Pollock about what Carl said. As we thought through the work our students had given us throughout the year, we knew it was true. For years I had made a big point of teaching setting over the year. Whether we were writing fiction or poetry, studying craft or revision I continually hammered home the point that place was important. But when I looked back at the past year, I saw that I had not focused on it. It was quite clear as I laid out the independent work I received from my students. Piece after piece paid cursory attention to setting, nothing like the pieces I had seen during the years where it had been a major thread in my teaching. But I *had* really worked on finding a strong sense of one's own voice and style as a writer. Again, as I laid out the independent pieces side by side I noticed that in everything from letters to cookbooks there was a style in each voice that was unique to that writer. It was fabulous to see unequivocal proof that students had absorbed my teaching to the point that it was a regular part of their writing.

As Kate and I talked further about it, we realized that there were many times when we thought students had mastered a skill or technique only to discover that the mastery we expected was suspiciously missing from most of their independent work. We were able think through our next year's teaching plans based on our understanding of where our teaching was stronger or weaker from the independent writing litmus test.

Some things we kept in mind as we looked through the students' writing included:

- Trends we noticed across pieces. What were some good habits they had developed? What were some not so good ones?
- Were students publishing in genres we had taught earlier in the year? How much of that teaching did they apply?
- What surprised us about the students' work as a whole?

In addition to looking at students writing to assess our teaching, it is also helpful to be reflective about students' general attitudes—one of the aspects of teaching I value the most. Since I sincerely love writing, I hoped that the students would have at least some of that tendency as well. I thought about whether students had a generally positive attitude about writing, and whether I had noticed an improvement in those attitudes since the fall. It was nice for me to be able to note that for most of the class writing had become more fun and a part of the day they sincerely looked forward to. Oscar, who had proclaimed, "I hate writing!" on his beginning of the year assessment happily discussed his plans for his next writing piece.

I think it's helpful to take our own attitudes into account as well. Did I enjoy teaching writing this year? What did I enjoy most? Least? By thinking honestly about those questions I make next year's teaching effective for the students as well as myself. The old saying, "If Mama's not happy, no one's happy" applies to the classroom family as well. I know if I am happy with how things are going, my students are more likely to be happy too.

Assessing Our Students

In addition to the groundbreaking notion that we could gain a sense of our writing teaching effectiveness across the year by looking closely at independently published pieces, Kate and I knew we could also use the students' independent pieces to holistically assess our students. We knew there were certain things we could expect to see in each student's work while also looking for goals we had set for individual students.

For example, I expected everyone in my class to have improved their editing skills, mastered a few revision techniques, regularly used a mentor, shown expertise at writing in at least one genre, shown evidence of clear structure, and exhibited a strong sense of voice and style. When I looked at my students' work by and large this was the case. Except for that giant gaping hole (to me, anyway) of use of setting in writing, my expectations for my students and what they had succeeded in doing seemed to be consistent.

In September I had specific goals for each student. For Nili, I had hoped she would finish some pieces without my input. I wanted Aaron to actually enjoy writing—not really an academic goal, but one I wanted nonetheless. My goal for Oscar was to write pieces that were important to him and to share with the world the stories he wanted to share. I wanted Kenya to let loose a little and write with abandon without getting snagged on tricky spelling words and perfect punctuation. I wanted Aidan to concentrate a little, to see if there was something in the literary world that would hold his attention as much as a football game did. My goal for Ruthie was to better understand her writing process and share with others that process.

When I looked at them in June it was interesting to see how those goals panned out.

Nili had published seven pieces independently. Among them were a picture book, a class newspaper, and a poetry anthology. She had published most of them with very little assistance from me. Instead she relied on Karen Hesse's mentorship and the support of her writing club.

Aaron had published several pieces independently over the course of the year. Among them was a mystery short story and a poetry anthology. One night he sent me e-mail at 10:30 P.M. to tell me he was just getting to bed because he had been writing and he couldn't sleep because he was so lost in his story.

Oscar had his article on the Giants rookie, the "Super Guy" comic book series, and a picture book about motorcycles to his credit. He turned an early draft of his feature article into a small nonfiction picture book on wolves, "because people think they're all bad and want to kill them, but they're not bad."

Aidan finished his very popular cookbook and went on to write song lyrics for his acapella band. Ruthie became one of the most talkative writers during whole-class discussions, and even taught a seminar on ways to use a writer's notebook, while managing to work on her Magic Marbor series as well.

Even though Kenya never got to finish her play, she did discover something that could combine her love of color and drama. She created a series of books

---

MAY

HAPPY BIRTHDAY TO MEATBALLS

In May is my birthday and these are delicious presents.

2 lbs. ground beef

2 small cans Arturo tomato sauce

2 one-pound cans whole cranberries

1 small onion

4 slices crestless white bread soaked in milk

1 can water

Salt and pepper

2 tbls. butter

White rice

Combine meat, bread, milk, salt and pepper, and onion. Make small meatballs, about one

inch in diameter. Brown in butter in large skillet. Add sauce and cook for ½ hour or more.

Serve over white rice.

Figure 6–1a Excerpts from a Student's Cookbook

using Polaroid photographs of her posed dolls and stuffed animals to illustrate her stories.

Each of us has goals for our class as a whole, as well as goals for individual students. It is helpful to lay those side by side and try to determine how the majority of the class, as well as each individual, fits into our planned goals and expectations. One way to do that is to decide what to expect for different teaching points across the year. So, for example, what do I expect from students' writers' notebooks in October when we have only looked at them closely during our study of living like a writer, as compared to January after we have completed our mini-study of notebooks, as compared to June when we should have some mastery? The chart on pages 158–160 lists my expectations for my students during those three points in the year in those key elements of independence. While I surely don't

OCTOBER

THE GREAT PUMPKIN BREAD

The only reason the Great Pumpkin rises is because he smells the Great Pumpkin Bread as it rises too. You can't blame him because this moist, marvelous loaf of bread will attract anyone…or anything!

1 ½ c. sugar

1 tsp. baking soda

¾ tsp. salt

¼ tsp. baking powder

½ tsp. cloves

½ tsp. cinnamon

½ tsp. nutmeg

½ tsp. allspice

1 2/3 c. flour

½ c. vegetable oil

½ c. water

1 c. canned pumpkin

2 eggs

In a large bowl mix ingredients in the order given. Pour batter into a well-greased 9"x5" loaf pan. Bake at 325* for 1 ½ hours or until a toothpick inserted in the center comes out clean.

Figure 6–1b Excerpts from a Student's Cookbook

expect every student to have met every expectation by the month I chose to check in, it helps to get a general idea of the way I hope my students will be advancing (give or take a month or two).

Independence offers us a way to look at work once removed from our teaching and see how our teaching has affected students' work. True, the fact that we actually get to read these pieces and that the idea for writing them might have been generated in the classroom makes the assessment a little less authentic. But the

---

NOVEMBER

WISH FOR MORE GINGER SNAPS

When the turkey is gone and you are about to snap the wishbone, you'll be wishing for these crunchy ginger snaps for dessert.

¾ c. margarine

1 c. sugar plus ½ c. to roll in dough

¼ c. light molasses

1 egg, beaten

2 c. flour

¼ tsp. salt

2 tsp. baking soda

1 tsp. cinnamon

1 tsp. cloves

1 tsp. ginger

Cream margarine and sugar, add molasses and egg, and beat well. Add sifted dry ingredients; mix well. Wrap in waxed paper and put into refrigerator overnight. Then roll in small balls, roll in sugar. Place two inches apart on greased cookie sheets. Bake at 375* for 8 minutes or less. Cool on cookie rack.

Figure 6–1c Excerpts from a Student's Cookbook

truest assessment of our teaching would require waiting until students are all grown up and living on their own; few of us would have the patience for that.

Student Self-Assessment

Since I was honest with my students from the beginning of the year about my teaching brain, it stands to reason that I would be open about assessment as well. All year we had been collecting work in folders. Not all the work was related to writing, but much of it was. As the year drew to a close I gathered up the folders and talked about one of our last projects—self-assessing through portfolios.

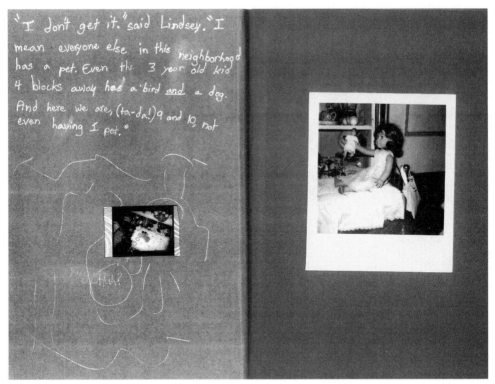

"I don't get it." said Lindsey. "I mean everyone else in this neighborhood has a pet. Even the 3 year old kid 4 blocks away has a bird and a dog. And here we are, (ta-da!) 9 and 10, not even having I pet."

Figure 6–2a Excerpts from a Student's Picture Book Series

We talked about how artists keep portfolios as a way of showing people the very best work they can do, as well as to show the variety of possible projects. For my class the portfolios had multiple purposes. They were a way to show off their work to others, certainly. They were also a way for me to get a sense of their general attitudes about the year, as well as their attitudes about their own work: what they thought they did well, and what they left out. The portfolios also allow the students to take some time to assess their own learning in a thoughtful way by looking at their year in fourth grade as a whole, all the subjects and months laid out.

There are countless ways for students' portfolios to be compiled and reflected upon. The way my students put together their portfolios was probably at the simplest end of the portfolio spectrum.

The students looked through all the work in their folders from over the year. I asked them to pick their best pieces and the ones they thought best represented their abilities. Students talked over their decisions with classmates then chose the way they wanted to reflect on their work. Students had a choice between three

Figure 6–2b Excerpts from a Student's Picture Book Series

possible ways to reflect: a letter, a long-answer questionnaire, or a short-answer questionnaire. It was fascinating to watch them painstakingly choose the pieces that they thought best exemplified their body of work in fourth grade. Most students surprised me with their choices. Almost without exception students chose at least one independently published piece. What they had to say about their pieces was very telling.

Aidan chose a historical fiction piece from his portfolio and wrote, "I think it taught me how to nurture a little. At least in a pretty good way. And it got me used to writing in this class. And writing independent pieces, because not everyone did the same genre . . . I didn't think it was that great, but it's what I wrote before I learned all the writing tecneques [sic] so it was good for what I knew then."

Nili chose a realistic fiction piece called "The Journey" and said something important about how independent pieces can be balanced and affected by other studies when she wrote, "I was doing the punctuation study while I was doing this piece so I tried to learn a lot from the punctuation. I used elipses [sic], semicolons, commas, periods, quotes and more punctuation."

	October	January	June
Independently planning and completing writing pieces	With teacher and peer support: • Create project proposals • Plan deadlines and pace projects • Monitor for quality, content and genre • Keep track of ideas for future projects • Capable of proficient use of non-human resources (dictionary, thesaurus, grammar guides, etc.)	With some teacher and more peer support: • Create project proposals • Plan deadlines and pace projects • Monitor for quality, content and genre • Keep track of ideas for future projects • Capable of proficient use of non-human resources (dictionary, thesaurus, grammar guides, etc.) • Balance working on concurrent projects (independent and whole class)	With limited teacher and some peer support: • Create project proposals • Plan deadlines and pace projects • Monitor for quality, content and genre • Keep track of ideas for future projects • Capable of proficient use of non-human resources (dictionary, thesaurus, grammar guides, etc.) • Balance working on concurrent projects (independent and whole class) • Able to envision working successfully without teacher support over summer months
Choosing and using mentor authors/texts	With teacher and peer support: • Able to identify mentor author and/or text which would be most useful for supporting independent project • Studies mentor text and notices good writing techniques • Proficient use of crafting strategies noticed in mentor text	With some teacher and peer support: • Able to identify mentor author and/or text which would be most useful for supporting independent project • Studies mentor text and notices good writing techniques • Proficient use of crafting strategies noticed in mentor text • Use of mentors an instinctive part of writing process	With limited teacher and peer support: • Able to identify mentor author and/or text which would be most useful for supporting independent project • Studies mentor text and notices good writing techniques • Proficient use of crafting strategies noticed in mentor text • Use of mentors an instinctive part of writing process • Has personal collection of favorite mentors that reflect the students' writing style and habits

	With teacher and peer support:	After whole-class study of notebooks, with some teacher and peer support:	With limited teacher and peer support:
Using writer's notebook in support of independent work	• Begin to develop personalized methods of notebook keeping • Able to apply whole-class notebook techniques to independent project notebook work • Uses notebook in a variety of ways such as: note-taking, jotting, charts, sketches, and so on that support projects.	• Develop and maintain personalized methods of notebook keeping • Able to apply whole-class notebook techniques to independent project notebook work • Uses notebook in a variety of ways such as: note taking, jotting, charts, sketches, and so on that support projects • Understand connection between notebook writing and productiveness in independent work • Has additional notebooks earmarked for distinct purposes (optional)	• Develop and maintain personalized methods of notebook keeping • Able to apply whole-class notebook techniques to independent project notebook work • Uses notebook in a variety of ways such as: note taking, jotting, charts, sketches, and so on that support projects • Understand connection between notebook writing and productiveness in independent work • Has additional notebooks earmarked for distinct purposes (optional) • Plans for summer and future notebook work are connected to independent projects
	With teacher support:	With some teacher support:	With limited teacher support:
Building and sustaining a writing community	• Able to positively support fellow writers in small and large group situations • Proficient at discussing independent work successes and needs	• Able to positively support fellow writers in small and large group situations • Proficient at discussing independent work successes and needs • Listens attentively and learns from fellow writers	• Able to positively support fellow writers in small and large group situations • Proficient at discussing independent work successes and needs • Listens attentively and learns from fellow writers • Maintains an ongoing writing relationship with at least one other person

Continued on next page

	October	January	June
Building and sustaining a writing community (*continued*)	• Listens attentively and learns from fellow writers • Maintains an ongoing writing relationship with at least one other person	• Maintains an ongoing writing relationship with at least one other person • Asks for and offers writing assistance as needed • Criticizes other writers' work with kindness and honesty in a way that is helpful to the writer • Weighs criticism from other writers and determines its usefulness in own work in a positive way	• Criticizes other writers' work with kindness and honesty in a way that is helpful to the writer • Weighs criticism from other writers and determines its usefulness in own work in a positive way • Asks for and offers writing assistance as needed, including attending or giving seminars, establishing book clubs, and contributing to class in other ways • Plans for reconnection with writing partner or club in the future
Connecting independent writing to whole-class curriculum	With teacher and peer support: • Connects writing process across units of study to the process that occurs in independent writing • Meets independently set deadlines as frequently as teacher-set deadlines	With some teacher and peer support: • Connects writing process across units of study to the process that occurs in independent writing • Meets independently set deadlines as frequently as teacher-set deadlines • Uses skills and techniques learned during whole class studies while writing independent pieces with proficiency	With limited teacher and peer support: • Connects writing process across units of study to the process that occurs in independent writing • Meets independently set deadlines as frequently as teacher-set deadlines • Uses skills and techniques learned during whole class studies while writing independent pieces with proficiency • Creates at least one independent piece in a genre that was part of a whole-class study

The portfolios were a helpful self-assessment tool for the students because they had been reflecting on and assessing their work all year long. Every whole-class writing piece, every independently published piece, and virtually every other academic area had been assessed by the students themselves as well as by me all year long. I know there are many books that talk about the value of organic assessment as well as the many advantages that come from students' self-assessment. From my experience, the act of self-assessment, of realizing one's abilities, strengths, and weaknesses is a crucial building block for students as they develop their independence. (See Figures 6–3 to 6–8.)

Time to Show Off with PORTFOLIOS!

Directions:

1. Look through all your folders, and choose 4 – 6 pieces that you think either show how much you've grown as a 4th grader *or* are your very best work. **Make sure at least 3 different subjects are represented.** (For example: 2 writing pieces, one reading response, a Plimoth Journal would be a great collection.)

2. Put all your other work in your homework folder to take home.

3. Now spread out the pieces you chose. Take a good look at them. Pat yourself on the back then . . .

4. Choose how you are going to reflect on your work this year as a 4th grader. You can either: <u>write a letter</u> to Colleen & Jen *or* fill out a <u>long answer</u> questionnaire *or* fill out a <u>short answer</u> questionnaire.

5. Follow the directions on the "Personal Reflection" Sheet. Then, put all your pieces back in your portfolio with your finished letter or questionnaire on top.

6. Celebrate! You have officially collected all your best work from 4th grade and can show it off to anyone you want!

Figure 6–3 Portfolio Directions

Personal Reflection on Your 4ᵗʰ Grade Portfolio

This is your chance to show how well you think and write about your own learning. You have three choices for how to reflect on your work:

1. **The Letter:** You will write a letter to Colleen & Jen and talk about how your work in your portfolio shows how much you have grown and changed in 4ᵗʰ grade. The letter will include:
   - An introduction that tells us how you have learned and grown as a learner and thinker over this past year.
   - A short paragraph for *each* piece of work you have chosen to include in your portfolio. In those paragraphs you will explain what you have learned from creating those pieces.
   - A conclusion talking about the goals you have for yourself as a learner and thinker, based on the work you have done on your portfolio.

2. **The Long Answer:** You will fill out a questionnaire with questions about the work you chose for your portfolio. These will be longer answers. The questions are basically the same as the ones you would write about in the letter.

3. **The Short Answer:** You will fill out a questionnaire with questions about the work you chose for your portfolio. These will be shorter answers. The questions are basically the same as the ones you would write about in the letter.

Figure 6–4 Guidelines for Portfolio

Celebration

In the midst of all this assessment it was easy for me to dismiss the importance of celebration. We had begun the year with a toast after our first publication. As we stood with our glasses raised to the writing pieces hung on the bulletin board we had hopes of where we would be able to go, but no possible way of knowing what the future held in store. When I looked back at that moment I realized we needed to celebrate even more in June.

Personal Reflection: SHORT ANSWER

You have chosen to answer questions about your portfolio! This is your chance to talk about how much you have grown and changed in the 4th grade. Take some time to look through your portfolio and think about the choices that you have made before you answer the questions below.

1. What is one way that you have grown as a learner this year? How have you improved?

_____

_____

_____

2. What is another way that you have grown as a learner this year? How have you improved?

_____

_____

_____

3. What is the **first** piece in your portfolio? (Title, subject, etc.)

_____

Why did you choose it?

_____

_____

4. What is the **second** piece in your portfolio? (Title, subject, etc.)

_____

Why did you choose it?

_____

_____

5. What is the **third** piece in your portfolio? (Title, subject, etc.)

Figure 6–5 Personal Reflection—Short Answer

Why did you choose it?

_____

_____

6. What is the **fourth** piece in your portfolio? (Title, subject, etc.)

_____

Why did you choose it?

_____

_____

7. What is the **fifth** piece in your portfolio? (Title, subject, etc.)

_____

Why did you choose it?

_____

_____

8. Looking at all the pieces you have you should notice some things you can work on, or improve. What is one goal you have after looking through your portfolio?

_____

_____

What is another goal you have after looking through your portfolio?

9. What did you like *best* about doing your portfolio?

_____

_____

10. What did you like *least* about doing your portfolio?

_____

_____

Figure 6–5 Continued

Personal Reflection: LONG ANSWER

You have chosen to answer questions about your portfolio! This is your chance to talk about how much you have grown and changed in the 4th grade. Take some time to look through your portfolio and think about the choices that you have made before you answer the questions below.

1. What are two ways you have grown as a learner and thinker this year in 4th grade? Be specific.

A. _____

_____

_____

_____

_____

B. _____

_____

_____

_____

_____

2. Look at your 1st piece in your portfolio. What is it? (Title, subject, genre, etc.)

_____

What did you learn from creating it?

_____

_____

_____

_____

Why did you choose it?

_____

_____

_____

3. Look at your 2nd piece in your portfolio. What is it? (Title, subject, genre, etc.)

Figure 6–6 Personal Reflection—Long Answer

What did you learn from creating it?

_____

_____

_____

_____

_____

Why did you choose it?

_____

_____

_____

_____

4. Look at your 3ʳᵈ piece in your portfolio. What is it? (Title, subject, genre, etc.)

_____

What did you learn from creating it?

_____

_____

_____

_____

_____

Why did you choose it?

_____

_____

_____

_____

5. Look at your 4ᵗʰ piece in your portfolio. What is it? (Title, subject, genre, etc.)

_____

What did you learn from creating it?

_____

_____

_____

_____

Figure 6–6 Continued

Why did you choose it?

_____

_____

_____

_____

6. Look at your 5th piece in your portfolio. What is it? (Title, subject, genre, etc.)

_____

What did you learn from creating it?

_____

_____

_____

_____

_____

Why did you choose it?

_____

_____

_____

_____

7. What goals do you have for yourself as a thinker and learner based on what work you have done on your portfolio? Describe.

_____

_____

_____

_____

_____

_____

_____

8. Anything else to add?

_____

_____

_____

_____

Figure 6–6 Continued

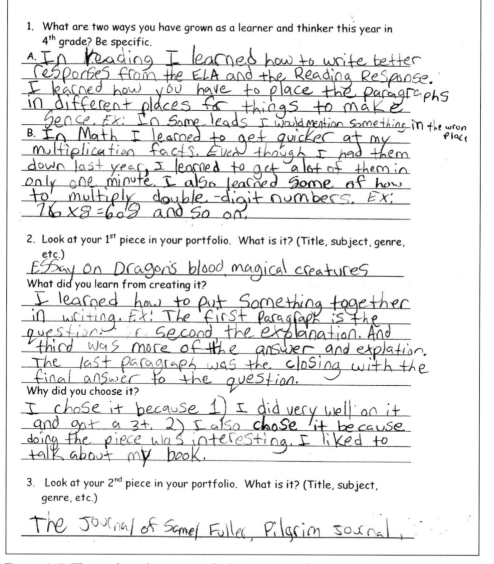

Personal Reflection: LONG ANSWER

You have chosen to answer questions about your portfolio! This is your chance to talk about how much you have grown and changed in the 4th grade. Take some time to look through your portfolio and think about the choices that you have made before you answer the questions below.

1. What are two ways you have grown as a learner and thinker this year in 4th grade? Be specific.

A. In reading I learned how to write better responses from the ELA and the Reading Response. I learned how you have to place the paragraphs in different places for things to make sence. Ex: In some leads I would mention something in the wrong place

B. In Math I learned to get quicker at my multiplication facts. Even though I had them down last year, I learned to get a lot of them in only one minute. I also learned some of how to multiply double-digit numbers. Ex: 16 x 8 = 60'8 and so on.

2. Look at your 1st piece in your portfolio. What is it? (Title, subject, genre, etc.)

Essay on Dragon's blood magical creatures

What did you learn from creating it?

I learned how to put something together in writing. Ex: The first paragraph is the question. The second the explanation. And third was more of the answer and explation. The last paragraph was the closing with the final answer to the question.

Why did you choose it?

I chose it because 1) I did very well on it and got a 3+. 2) I also choose it because doing the piece was interesting. I liked to talk about my book.

3. Look at your 2nd piece in your portfolio. What is it? (Title, subject, genre, etc.)

The Journal of Samel Fuller, Pilgrim Journal.

Figure 6–7 This student chose to use the Long Answer form.

What did you learn from creating it?

I learned what life was like for a pilgrim Man in 1620 and later. I also learned Some pilgrim history, and I also learned all the bad and good things that happened on the Mayflower, and Some on the Speedwell.

Why did you choose it?

I chose it because I enjoyed writing in a journal and Seeing what life was like as a Man. I also chose it because it was interesting using old words like 'Tis and cast and up-grown.

4. Look at your 3rd piece in your portfolio. What is it? (Title, subject, genre, etc.)

The Journey, Realistic Fiction, independent.

What did you learn from creating it?

I was doing the punctuation Study while I was doing this piece, So I tried to learn a lot from the punctuation. and So I used elipses, semi-colans, commas, periods, quotes, and more punctuation.

Why did you choose it?

I chose this piece because I've wanted to write Something in perspective of a little girl who is writing in her diary about her life.

5. Look at your 4th piece in your portfolio. What is it? (Title, subject, genre, etc.)

The Human Body..., Feature Article.

What did you learn from creating it?

I learned Some cool facts about the Human body. Ex: In one Minute blood travels 40 feet. I also learned alot of People pick their nose and eat their boogers. Ex: 26 out of 29 people picked their nose.

Figure 6–7 Continued

Why did you choose it?

I chose it because I liked making the Feature Article and writing down all the grass and cool facts because I liked breading stuff like that myself.

6. Look at your 5th piece in your portfolio. What is it? (Title, subject, genre, etc.)

Realistic Fiction, The Losers winnings.

What did you learn from creating it?

I learned how to make a realistic character that doesn't exist but is real. I also learned how to make a realistic setting that was partly real. I used the B63 bus and a new setting, a sports games park that I made up.

Why did you choose it?

I chose it because I did a good job on it. I got a 4. And, I liked doing the piece because I got to make up anything I wanted that was realistic.

7. What goals do you have for yourself as a thinker and learner based on what work you have done on your portfolio? Describe.

I want to get better at getting writing essays.

8. Anything else to add?

Not really.

Figure 6–7 Continued

I wanted to make sure my students had an opportunity to celebrate not only all their hard work, but also the relationships they built together. It was important to take the time to acknowledge their hard work so that they were to able to add to their growth in self-esteem, share their accomplishments with family and friends, and have fun while doing it. Besides all that, I must admit I even feel more compelled to work hard when I was rewarded in some way. A celebration is certainly a kind of reward.

Dear Coleen and Jen,

I think I have really grown as a fourth grader. For a example, in writing I learned how to make an exellent web, and my writing has really improved. So has my math. I am really good at it now.

My ideas about American Indians have really changed. I always thought that all of them were like the ones that lived in Wigwams and Longhouses, or that were from the movie, Peter Pan. Now, I know all about what really went on and what they really were like.

My fantasy essay (I learned) was really awesome. I was really happy. By writing it, I found out that not only I am a good essay writer, I also learnd how to write essays.

My feature article helped me figure out that they weren't nonfiction books. It helped me learn more about Barbies, and how to write a feature article and plan it. It also helped me tell the difference between an Interview and a survey.

My independent writing peice, The Basement, helped me write poems better. It also expressed my feelings about the basement in my house.

My math sheet about the window shades helped me learn more in math. It also helped me learn that even though both things may not be showing, you can count one thing, and always estimate the other to be about the same.

My realistic fiction piece helped me with a lot of things. It helped me nurture better, revise better, and write better. It was my favorite peice of the whole year.

My goals are to do better at math writing, and start work early and finish early so I won't have to worry about it in my spare time.

Figure 6–8 This student chose to write a letter.

Since I planned the first celebration, I thought it only fitting that the students plan our last. It seemed a perfect tribute to their independence. I announced to the students that they would be in charge of our final celebration. I told them it would probably work best if they were in committees. The committees they joined were:

- *Invitations & Programs.* This committee was responsible for creating invitations for all our class families as well as other school community members. They also created a program for the event, which they passed out on the day of the celebration
- *Decorations.* They were responsible for our welcome sign, creating paper chains, blowing up balloons, and generally making the classroom festive for the big occasion.
- *Refreshments.* They created a menu of refreshments, then met before the big day to prepare their fruit salad, cookies, and punch. They also served our guests.
- *Entertainment.* They planned how we kept our guests entertained. They chose two songs they wanted the class to sing and the writing they wanted to be read, and they wrote a thank you speech to thank the grownups who supported them.
- *Booths.* They organized the work they wanted displayed on tables and created large colorful signs identifying the materials. These tables, also called booths, displayed the students' portfolios, social studies work, our recently completed photo essays, as well as our independent pieces.

I gave the students a few class periods to work with their committees as well as a period for final set up and rehearsal.

When our guests arrived, greeted at the door by students and their handmade program, they could already tell this was an independent bunch. Everything from the songs that they sung to the balloons that were hung high enough for a fourth grader but too low for a grandfather to walk under, was planned and realized by the students. There are many ways to celebrate the end of the year in writing. My students celebrated working together by working together. It was by far my favorite writing celebration.

Plans for the Summer, Plans for a Lifetime

When the celebration was over, the portfolios had been packed up, and it was just us left in our classroom that was already being dismantled, we gathered on the rug to talk. We sat in the circle we always sat in when we met as a writing colony. Now there was a new kind of energy in the space we shared together; we were more like colleagues, myself included, than we had ever been.

"This isn't really going to be a mini-lesson right now. But this is our last writing workshop," I began. A few sad glances were exchanged at the announcement.

"We did a lot of writing this year. The most important writing to me was the stuff you did independently. Those pieces showed me what you were really capable of accomplishing when there were no teachers around to help you. I've told you all along that my goal for you was to become the kinds of people who write all your life. That starts with this summer," I said.

Some students groaned good-naturedly. "We're going to spend a little time thinking about what kind of writing we're planning on doing this summer. I know I have a book I need to finish writing, and I want to write a letter to the mayor about making ferrets legal in New York City. You might want to continue with a project you started this year, like a series. Or maybe you want to finish a project you didn't have time to finish during the school year. I know Kenya has plans to finish her play." I gave the students a chance to turn and talk to somebody sitting near them about possible summer plans before I went on.

"Now I want you to imagine a crystal ball that can see into the future. What kind of writing do you imagine yourself doing later, in the far future? I'm not saying you're all going to become novelists or people who write picture books. But I think that almost any job you do requires writing. Lawyers write something called legal briefs. Veterinarians write medical reports. Not to mention letters to friends, poems for special occasions that you might also want to write," I said. I gave them a chance to talk to each other again.

When everyone seemed to have a few ideas I said, "We're going to make a little contract with ourselves right now. We're not short-term writers in this room. We're in it for the long haul. I want everyone to pull out his or her writer's notebook and make a 't-chart'. One column can be titled 'Summer Writing Plans' and the other can be called, 'Far Future Writing Plans.'"

Students went off to fill out their charts. Then a few students wanted to share their plans. Aidan said, "Over the summer I want to write a few more songs for my band. For the far future I want to write more about football since I plan to be a football player."

Oscar liked that idea and jotted it down in his notebook before volunteering, "Over the summer I want to write another article about the Giants. I don't know about my far future yet."

Aaron smiled, "I'm going to start a novel over the summer. I don't know if I'll finish it, but I'm going to start it. I also know in my far future I want to write more novels because I'm going to be a writer."

I had no idea how many of their plans would come into being as we all sat together one last time. I supposed it didn't really matter though. They had learned to become more independent that year. They had created plays, cookbooks, newspapers, magazines, picture books, poetry, comic books, short stories, science fiction,

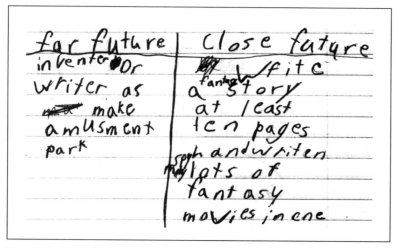

Figure 6–9 Student's Writing Plans for the Close Future and the Far Future

mysteries, and even started a novel or two. Just that morning, Aidan had slipped me a cassette tape. "There's three songs that Eric, Jeffrey and I recorded last night. You know the songs we've been working on in the hallway all month? You just got to promise not to play it until we all leave," he said.

Yes, I could safely say, as much as my superstitious teaching head was afraid to admit it (knock on wood), I had taught them to lead writing lives that were more independent than they had been before they entered my classroom.

It didn't matter if they made good on all of their plans for the summer, all of their plans for their future. As a writer friend taught me—once a person has learned to write independently she stops being called an independent writer.

She is simply a writer.

Afterword

I never liked the last day of school.

I hated saying good-bye to my students. I could not stand the feelings of self-doubt I always had as I watched them walk out of the school building into the June sunlight. I wondered if I had taught everything I should have taught, helped every student I could have helped. I questioned whether I had affected any of the kids in any measurable way.

I was hot, sweaty and smudged with dust despite the air conditioner working away behind me. I wallowed in I-hate-the-last-day-of-school feelings. The students had left hours ago, and I dealt with the depressing task of packing up the boxes, tearing down the bulletin boards and trashing the work students had decided they didn't want to keep. I tried to focus on the summer days ahead, but instead found it much more pleasurable to pick at my insecurities. After all, I would have all summer to feel relaxed and satisfied.

Aaron peeked his head through the classroom door. He was a student from the last year's class. I was surprised to see him since most recent fifth grade graduates tended not to hang around their elementary school longer than they had to.

"I have something for you," he said. He was holding a stack of white papers held together with a large binder clip. He looked nervous.

I wiped my hands on my shorts and reached for it.

"It's the beginning of my novel. The first sixty-five pages. I thought maybe you'd like to read it," he said. He blushed.

I cleared my throat. I wanted to throw my arms around him and say, "A novel! That's amazing! I can't believe you're working on a novel." But I knew that would convey a sense of disbelief and shock that I knew would embarrass him more than make him happy. I knew that instead I should act as I would with another writer, a colleague. Which he was, now that he was gone from elementary school and headed off to middle school.

"Great," I said instead, taking the huge stack of papers into my hands. "I can hardly wait to read it."

Bibliography

Anderson, Carl. 2000. *How's It Going? A Practical Guide to Conferring with Students.* Portsmouth, NH: Heinemann.

Calkins, Lucy. 1994. *The Art of Teaching Writing.* Portsmouth, NH: Heinemann.

Cambourne, Brian, and Jan Turnbill. 1981. *Coping with Chaos.* Portsmouth, NH: Heinemann.

Fletcher, Ralph. 1996. *Breathing in, Breathing Out: Keeping a Writer's Notebook.* Portsmouth, NH: Heinemann.

———. 1996. *A Writer's Notebook: Unlocking the Writer Within You.* New York: Avon Books.

———. 1999. *Live Writing: Breathing Life into Your Words.* New York: Avon.

———. 2000. *How Writers Work: Finding a Process That Works for You.* New York: Harper Collins.

Fletcher, Ralph, and JoAnn Portalupi. 2001. *Writing Workshop: The Essential Guide.* Portsmouth, NH: Heinemann.

Graham, Paula, ed. 1999. *Speaking of Journals: Children's Book Writers Talk About Their Diaries, Notebooks and Sketchbooks.* Honesdale, PA: Boyds Mill Press.

Graves, Donald. 1994. *A Fresh Look at Writing.* Portsmouth, NH: Heinemann.

Hesse, Karen. 1998. *Just Juice.* New York: Scholastic.

Kemper, Dave, Ruth Nathan, and Patrick Sebranek. 1995. *Writer's Express:* A Handbook for young Writers, Thinkers and Learners. Boston: Houghton Mifflin.

Locker, Thomas. 1997. *Water Dance.* San Diego, CA: Harcourt Brace.

Pilkey, Dav. 1999. *Captain Underpants and the Attack of the Talking Toilets: An Epic Novel.* New York: Scholastic.

Ray, Katie Wood. 1999. *Wondrous Words: Writers and Writing in the Elementary Classroom.* Urbana, IL: NCTE.

———. 2001. *The Writing Workshop: Working Through the Hard Parts (And They're All Hard Parts).* Urbana, IL: NCTE.

————. 2002. *What You Know by Heart: How to Develop Curriculum for Your Writing Workshop.* Portsmouth, NH: Heinemann.

Rylant, Cynthia. 1998. *Scarecrow.* San Diego, CA: Harcourt Brace.

Thomas, Marlo, ed. 1997. *Free to Be . . . You and Me* PA: Running Press.

Wesner, David, Year. *The Three Pigs.* New York: Clarion.

Index

A

All Kinds of Minds, 136
All Those Secrets of the World, 49
Anderson, Carl, 62, 111, 150
Art of Teaching Writing, The, 20, 22
Assessment, 6
    checklist for, 19
    in classroom, 131–32
    end-of-year, 150, 151–55
    portfolios and, 156, 161
    purposes of, 16–20
    self-assessment by students, 9–10, 11, 12, 13,
        138, 155–61
    self-assessment by teachers, 150–51
    of year's progress, 158–60

B

Ballad of the Pirate Queens, The, 60
Belle, Jennifer, 96
Buddy system, 147
Bunting, Eve, 65

C

Calkins, Lucy, 2, 20, 22, 111
Cambourne, Brian, xv
Captain Underpants, 64, 66
Chicken Sunday, 60
Childhood's End, 132
Cisneros, Sandra, 57
Clarke, Arthur C., 132
Class deadline calendar, 124, 127
Classroom
    criticism in, 106, 108
    curriculum calendar in, 5–14

    at end of year, 149–74
    keeping track of work in, 123–30
    organization in, 142–45
    resources for, 145–46
    writing colonies in, 99–100
Community
    building, 119–21
    importance of, 118
    nonparticipants in, 118–19
Computers, to aid writing, 146
Conferences, 62–63
    importance of, 138–39
    peer, 30, 33
Conventions, writing, 26–28
Coping with Chaos, xv
Coville, Bruce, 79
Co-writing, 121
Crews, Donald, 57
Criticism, 101, 120
    in the classroom, 106, 108
    empathy in, 102
    teaching about, 109–10
Curriculum calendar, 6
    example of, 7–9
    goals of, 6
    individualized instruction in, 13–14
    offering choices in, 11–12

D

Dahl, Roald, 52
Deadlines, 29–30, 32, 93–94
    class, 124, 127
Devil's Arithmetic, The, 49
Dictation, 146

E

Elements of Style, 14

F

Fletcher, Ralph, xvi, 6, 22, 75
Flow charts, 143
Form, choice of, 29, 34
Free to Be You and Me, 62, 70
Fresh Look at Writing, A, 22

G

Gantos, Jack, 64, 76
Genre, 29, 34
   choice of, 62
   unfamiliar, 132–33, 135
George, Jean Craighead, 79, 87
Glasser, Perry, 93
Goals, setting, 6
Going Down, 96
Graves, Donald, 22
Greenfield, Eloise, 51, 53, 54

H

Henkes, Kevin, 51
Hesse, Karen, 51, 53, 65
High Maintenance, 96
Hinton, S. E., xv
Homework plans, 146
How Writers Work, xv, 6
How's It Going?, 62, 150

I

Ideas
   listing, 129
   nurturing, 29, 33
Independence, ix, xvi–xvii
   and community, 118–21
   fostering in children, 1–5
   fostering via curriculum calendar, 5–14
   study of, 58–59
   writing unit for, 14–36. *See also* Independence unit
Independence unit, 30–34
   assessment in, 16–20
   checklists in, 22
   conclusion and products of, 34–36, 37–43
   fundamentals in, 28
   review mini-unit, 139–40
   sample timeline for, 30–31
   studying the writerly life, 20–23
   supplies for, 14–15, 22
   writing conventions in, 26–28
Independent work
   grading of, 131–32
   keeping track of, by students, 129–30
   keeping track of, by teacher, 123–28
Independent writing
   calendars for, 129–31
   in curriculum, 134
   quality of, 135–40
Individualized Education Plans (IEPs), 142

J

Joey Pigza Swallowed the Key, 64, 76
Journals, 76
Julie, 87
Just Juice, 65

L

Length, of mentor texts, 62–63
Levine, Mel, 136
Lists, 144
Live Writing, xv
Locker, Thomas, 65, 66

M

The Math Curse, 111
Maus, 132
Mentors, 30, 34, 47, 137–38
   authors and their works as, 48–49, 57
   characteristics of, 61–62
   choice of, 49–51, 59–62, 64
   effective use of, 64–66
   flesh-and-blood, 47–48
   finding, 70
   fresh perspective of, 64
   teaching about, 51–62
   using, 64

N

Nia, Isoke, xvi, 4, 6, 7, 49, 51
Nurturing an idea, 29, 33

O

Organization
   of ideas, 143–45
   of materials, 142–43
Outlines, 144

P

Peer conferences, 30, 33
Personal rubrics, 138
Pilkey, Dav, 64, 66
Planning boxes, 143, 144
Pollock, Kate, 51, 52, 150, 151
Portalupi, JoAnn, 22
Portfolios, 156, 161
    guidelines for, 162
    personal reflections about, 163–71
Proposal sheet, 124, 125–26

Q

Quality
    of reading, 63
    of writing, 135–40
Quindlen, Anna, ii

R

Ray, Katie, xv, 4, 6, 22, 48, 49, 51, 70, 111
Reading, goals of, 48–49, 57
Reading and Writing Project (Columbia), 2, 4
Revision, teaching about, 138
Rowling, J. K., 64
Rylant, Cynthia, 51, 55, 57

S

Salinger, J. D., 93, 119
Salons, 98, 112–13
Scarecrow, 51, 55
Sczieska, John, 111
Self-assessment, 9–10
    checklist for, 10
    end-of-year, 155–61
    personal reflection, 163–71
    rubric for, 11, 12, 13, 138
    by teacher, 150–51
    teaching about, 30
Self-awareness, of students, 17
Seminars, 116–17
Simon, Seymour, 65
Sketching, 146
Smith, Emily, 113
Smith, Lane, 111
Soto, Gary, 51
Speaking of Journals, 76, 79
Spiegelman, Art. 132
Standardized testing, 133
Storyboards, 143–44

Struggling students
    who hate writing, 140–41
    with learning issues, 141–42
Strunk, William, 14
Subtopics, 145
Suslowitz, Bonni, 27

T

Taets, Jenifer, xi, 142, 143, 145, 146
Three Pigs, The, 111
Timelines, 144–45
Topic choice, 29
Turnbill, Jan, xvi

W

Water Dance, 66
We Had a Picnic This Sunday Past, 58, 76
Web, writer's, 143, 144
When I Was Little, 60
White, E. B., 14
Wiesner, David, 111
Wolves, 65
Wondrous Words, 48, 49, 51, 70
Woodson, Jacqueline, 21, 51, 53, 55, 58, 76
Writer's block, 73–74
Writer's Notebook, A, 22
Writer's notebooks, 30, 34
    comparing, 78–84
    described, 74–75
    dummy, 79
    expectations regarding, 91
    of experienced writers, 75–76
    mini-lessons about, 90
    models for, 79
    secret, 84–87
    student knowledge about, 78, 89–90
    as tools, 87
    uses for, 88–89
    variety of, 76–77
Writers
    as readers, 48
    solitude of, 96
    students as, 21–23
    studying lives of, 20–21
Writing
    as act of independence, ix, xvi–xvii
    computers to aid, 146
    conferences for, 62–63
    conventions of, 26–28

Writing, *continued*
 foundations of, 28
 importance of, ix–x
 individuality of techniques of, 6
 love of, xv–xvi, 17
 physical act of, 146–47
 problems of, 73–74
 as process, 17
 purposes of, 3
 troubleshooting, 64–65
Writing clubs, 98, 113–16
Writing colonies
 in the classroom, 99–100
 committing to, 96–97
 criticism in, 101–10
 described, 97–98
 help wanted and help offered in, 94–95, 120
 as human resource, 120
 levels of experience in, 94
 knowledge sharing in, 94
 peer accountability in, 93–94
 problem solving in, 94–95
 purposes of, 94–95, 97, 119–21
 responsibilities in, 120
 strength of, 120
 topics of discussion in, 100–1
Writing partnerships, 98, 111–12
 buddy system, 147

Writing process, 17
 teaching about, 29, 33
Writing Process Chart, 22, 124, 127–28
Writing Workshop, 22
Writing Workshop, The, 22
Writing workshops, xvi
 fostering independence in, 1–2, 4–5
 seminars in, 117
 and standardized testing, 133
 traditional structure of, 3

Y
Year's end
 assessment checklist for, 158–60
 assessment of students at, 150, 151
 celebration of, 162, 170
 and future plans, 172–75
 portfolios at, 156, 161
 self-assessment by students, 155–61
 self-assessment by teachers, 150–51
Yep, Laurence, 51, 52, 53
Yolen, Jane, 49, 51, 52, 60

Z
Zoltow, Charlotte, 65

Related writing titles from Heinemann

What You Know by Heart
How to Develop Curriculum for Your Writing Workshop
Katie Wood Ray

As Katie Ray shows, the most profound and effective curriculum can result from your own deep understanding of quality writing. Katie sprinkles special features throughout her book as helpful tips for thinking about your own writing workshop and curriculum development, including minilessons and "curriculum chunks"; "Thinking it Through" boxes with questions and things to try; "understandings" and strategies; notebook-keeping tips accompanied by Katie's own handwritten journal entries; transcripts of interviews with writers; and references for further reading.

0-325-00364-5 / 2002 / 208pp / $21.00

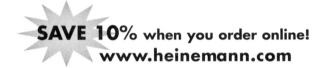

www.heinemann.com

To place an order, **call 800.225.5800** or **fax 603.431.2214.**

Related writing titles from Heinemann

Writing About Reading
From Book Talk to literary Essays, Grades 3–8
Janet Angelillo
Foreword by **Katie Wood Ray**

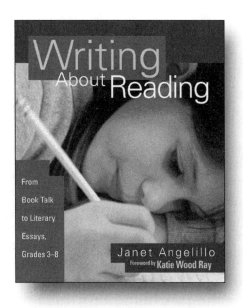

Janet Angelillo introduces us to an entirely new way of thinking about writing about reading. She shows us how to teach students to manage all the thinking and questioning that precedes their putting pen to paper. More than that, she offers us smarter ways to have students write about their reading that can last them a lifetime. She demonstrates how students' responses to reading can: start in a notebook, in conversation, or in a read aloud; lead to thinking guided by literary criticism; reflect deeper text analysis and honest writing processes; and result in a variety of popular genres—book reviews, author profiles, commentaries, editorials, and the literary essay.

She even includes tools for teaching—day-by-day units of study, teaching points, a sample minilesson, and lots of student examples—plus chapters on yearlong planning and assessment.

0-325-00578-8 / 2003 / 160pp / $18.00

Related writing titles from Heinemann

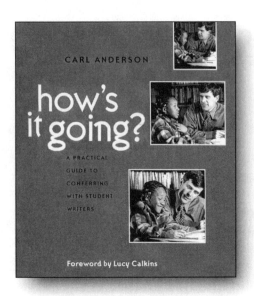

How's It Going?

A Practical Guide
to Conferring with
Student Writers
Carl Anderson
Foreword by **Lucy Calkins**

Our one-on-one talks with students
during writing workshop offer us
perfect opportunities to zero in on
what each student needs as a writer.
As Lead Staff Developer for the
Teachers College Reading and Writing
Project, carl Anderson has provided
hundreds of teachers with information
and confidence they need to make these complex conferences an effective
part of classroom practice. Finally, in *How's It Going?*, Anderson shares his
expertise with the rest of us.

0-325-00224-X / 2000 / 204pp / $22.00

Related writing titles from Heinemann

The Revision Toolbox
Teaching Techniques That Work
Georgia Heard

Using three main Revision Toolboxes—
Words, Structure, and Voice—Georgia
Heard offers dozens of specific revision
tools that inspire students to revisit their
work. In addition, Heard includes a
"Revision Lesson" for each tool to show
you how to teach that strategy; techniques to help students reread their
writing from different points of view;
conferring techniques to guide you when
instructing individual students; revision
examples from students and from Heard's
own writing; and "Revision-at-a-
Glance"—a quick-reference sheet for
students on every revision tool.

0-325-00460-9 / 2002 / 144pp / $17.00

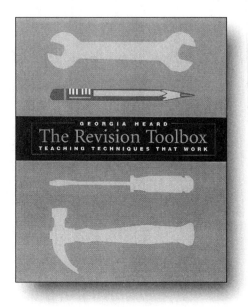

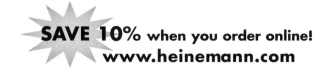

SAVE 10% when you order online!
www.heinemann.com

www.heinemann.com

To place an order, **call 800.225.5800** or **fax 603.431.2214.**